One Body Short of a Picnic

of a Picnic

CEDAR FISH CAMPGROUND SERIES: BOOK THREE

Leslie,
Have a
blast
reading!

CEDAR FISH
CAMPGROUND

Zoey Chase

Zoey Ch

PAGES TH
move

Book and Cover Design by Denise L. Murphy

PaGeS THaT *move*

Pittsburgh, PA
www.PagesThatMove.com

Printed in the United States of America

First Edition, 2020

ISBN 978-1-951873-06-6

Visit www.ZoeyChase.com and join my mailing list for freebies, occasional updates, and new release information.

Get a Cedar Fish Campground Full-Color Map!

Marked with important locations from book three:

- Murder Scene/Memorial
- Jerry and Mandy's Site
- New Horseshoe Pit
- Turtle Nest
- Turtle Crossing
- Thea and Nolan's Romantic Walk
- New Pond

Get the map and other freebies:

www.ZoeyChase.com/freebies

Find out more about how Gar came to Cedar Fish Campground in the short story "Fishy Beginnings."

When Gar's secret past is discovered, Thea must fight to keep her beloved pet.

Gar, a black Newfoundland puppy, mysteriously showed up at Cedar Fish Campground and became the perfect companion to heal Thea's grief-stricken, dog-loving heart. With such a serendipitous beginning, Thea never questioned the life Gar had before he found her. But one newspaper article could change everything.

Thea discovers a secret about Gar that could mean she loses him forever. With help from her ex-cop security guard, Nolan, and her quirky sidekick, Hennie, Thea must draw on her past to win the right to keep Gar before she loses another treasured pet.

FISHY BEGINNINGS is a short story that takes place after the events of *Between a Rock and a Deadly Place*, book one in the Cedar Fish Campground Series. If you love dogs or have ever lost a pet, you'll love this tale of hilarious animal antics and moments that will both break and warm your pet-loving heart.

CHAPTER 1

My stomach grumbled, making me feel sick in the sticky heat. I checked my watch again—12:20. Gar, my large Newfoundland puppy, looked up at me with a pleading expression. When I didn't get up, he stretched out on the cool cement floor of the vacant rec hall and sighed. My vendor meeting that was supposed to start at 12 should have ended by now, and I should be eating my lunch. I'd started having my meetings in the rec hall, rather than cramming into my tiny office, but sitting here bored and hungry in the heat made me reconsider.

The rec room contained only a few folding tables and chairs. I'd propped both doors open, but there wasn't much of a breeze. My eyes trailed the edges of the room. So much potential. I sighed. We were still in the fixing phase of things at Cedar Fish Campground. But the day would come when I could start remodeling and really do something with the huge, wasted space of the rec hall. I pictured game nights to balance out the bingo, and maybe some crafting events for kids. I could put some pool or ping-pong tables at one end, and it'd be great to add a snack bar. On my most ambitious days, I even saw myself leading a group of campers stretched out on mats, all of us doing yoga in the early morning. But I'd have to learn yoga first.

I picked up my walkie talkie and called to my employee, Sally, in the office. "Hey, have you seen Mr. Dorsey yet?" When no response came after several seconds, I called back. "Sally? Hello?"

Still nothing. I tried Curtis's channel next. He should be on security patrol and could check on the front of the campground for me. "Curtis, you there?"

When I got no response from him either, my heart rate spiked. I stood and looked out toward the office building next door. Gar jumped up as well, tongue lolling out and ready to play.

"Miss Thea?" Curtis's voice crackled over the airwaves.

I snatched my walkie to my mouth. "Yes, Curtis? I'm here."

"Seems we have a... situation near the front gate."

I gulped. With two recent murders in the campground, that could mean almost anything. "What sort of situation?"

"Maybe you could step out here a moment?"

I grabbed my travel mug of ice from the table and cautiously approached the rec hall door. Gar leapt through it ahead of me and ignored my command to come back. The bright noon sun beat down as I rounded the building.

Curtis, dashing as always in his old military uniform, stood with hands on hips in his usual hunch, inspecting an object on the ground. Sally stood beside him, her wavy red-brown hair almost glowing in the sunlight. They blocked my view of whatever our "situation" was. Since it didn't seem big enough to be a body, I relaxed and walked closer.

From under a nearby bush, three kitten heads peeked out in a row, also watching with intensity. Gar seemed oblivious to what was going on as he bounded in circles several feet away, batting at flowers and growling at anything that moved.

"What's going on?" I asked.

Curtis and Sally parted and gave me full view of the massive turtle sitting in the middle of the front drive.

I tilted my head at it. "Is that Rollie's turtle?" Rollie's General Store was a mile down the road, but giant turtles didn't seem all too common to me.

Curtis shook his head. "Smaller."

"It's definitely not Rollie's," Sally said. "My boys love to play with that turtle and they find shapes in his

shell designs. You know, like how kids do with clouds?"
She paused to make sure we followed.

"Cute," I said.

"Well, I know all of their favorite shapes, and this
turtle does not have the charging bear or the UFO. Also,
this turtle is much... scarier."

She had a point there. Three ridges of spiked shell
ran the length of the turtle. The spikes weren't sharp
enough to cut or stab, but they made for an intimidat-
ing show. The turtle that lived at Rollie's bore similar
spiked ridges, but less pronounced.

"So, if it's not the same turtle, do we have any idea
where it came from?" I asked.

"Must've come down the river and landed in the
lake," Curtis said.

"Will it go back?"

He shrugged.

"Can we move it from the road at least?"

He shook his head slowly. "Would *you* get near that
thing? Don't want to lose a hand."

I imagined that, in a showdown between Curtis and
the turtle, the turtle would come out faster.

Gar had finished his game of chase with a chipmunk
and dashed back to me. When he neared, he must've
smelled the turtle. He snarled and approached cautiously until he pressed his side against my legs.

I rubbed his head. "Just stay back, boy."

I stepped closer and bent down, reaching my hand hesitantly toward the middle of the turtle's shell.

"Bad idea," Nolan said.

I jumped at the sudden appearance of my handyman/security guard and fell on my butt. The turtle stuck its head out and hissed at me, its jaws stretching wide before snapping shut again. I scrambled to my feet and backed away. Gar barked, and that made the kittens bolt from their hiding spot. Gar took that as an invitation to chase after them.

Nolan laughed. "That thing could take your finger off in one bite. Were you trying to pet it?"

"No. I was trying to move it out of the way." I kept my eyes on the turtle that looked even more devilish with its pointy head visible.

"That's an alligator snapping turtle and probably weighs 60 pounds," Nolan said.

"If you know so much about it, why don't you go ahead and take care of it?" I patted his shoulder and gave him a curt smile.

"Yes, dear."

A car pulled in and stopped a few feet from us.

"My meeting is finally here anyway," I said. "Can you take Gar?"

Nolan glanced a few feet away where the puppy circled the kittens. He saluted to me and turned to the turtle.

Sally walked back to the office, muttering, "Wait until I tell my boys about this."

Curtis shuffled toward the wildlife pen.

Nolan inspected the turtle, scratching his beard in deep thought. I let my eyes linger a moment on the way his tan Cedar Fish Campground t-shirt stretched tight over his chest and biceps.

With a pleased sigh, I approached the car as the driver's window lowered.

"Hey Mark." I waved. "Sorry, we have a turtle situation. You can just cut through here to get to the parking lot in front of the office."

He nodded and drove where I pointed to the grass between the main entrance drive and the front parking lot.

Mark stepped out of his car wearing a short-sleeved button down and khakis. His blue tie was embroidered with two exploding fireworks in sparkling, metallic thread. The best part was the tiny LED lights that lit from the center of each starburst and blinked their way to the ends of the blast before starting over.

"We'll meet in the rec hall again."

He nodded and followed me past the turtle, Nolan, and Gar.

"You guys all ready for the big holiday?" he asked.

"Getting there," I said. "Lots of little details to finalize. Like this contract."

"Well, this won't take long, and I'll be out of your hair."

I gestured to the rec hall door, and he entered. We sat at the table where my copy of the final contract waited. "I checked everything over, and it all looks good to me."

"Great. And we're set on the initial and final payment amount?"

I slid a check out from under the contract. "I have the first payment right here."

It was more than I should probably spend on one event, but I hoped that the Fourth of July could keep business going. Things had picked up in the last month, but I worried that the second murder would lead to another crash in reservations. We still weren't very profitable, but we'd been slowly increasing. I'd decided to splurge on something huge to draw attention—a live fireworks display, set off right from our very own Dogwood Lake.

"Thank you." Mark took the check, folded it, and slid it into his shirt pocket. "All we need to do is sign."

We signed two copies of the contract, and he shook my hand. "I look forward to your event. It's going to be just as spectacular as you imagined."

"I'm counting on it." I followed him back outside.

Mark walked toward his car, and I returned to Nolan. Gar sat by his side, eyes trained on the turtle.

"You get it figured out?" The turtle stared back at me from the same position it was in before.

Nolan held up his phone, showing several photos of turtles. "I think it's a female."

"Okay, but how do we get her to move?"

"Either wait it out or try to lure her with some fish."

I poured a piece of ice into my mouth and chomped it. "Maybe we can call Enid and see if she has any ideas." I wasn't sure how Rollie's came to have a resident pet turtle, but the store's owner, Enid, was the only person I knew with giant-turtle experience.

Nolan nodded. "Was that the fireworks guy?"

"Yeah. I just signed the final contract."

"You went through with it?" Nolan put his phone in his pocket.

"Uhh, we decided this weeks ago when I gave him the deposit." I crossed my arms. Every time the Fourth of July event came up, Nolan took on some level of grumpiness about it. I'd ignored it, but his attitude grew worse the closer we got to July.

Nolan pressed his lips into a line and shook his head.

"What?" I asked.

"Told you this was a bad idea."

"Having a huge event to draw people to the campground? Why would that be a bad idea?"

"I mean the fireworks part," he explained. "Think about all that could go wrong. Did Mark even look into the ordinances for the area? I haven't seen a permit."

I put my hand on my hip. "That's because the permit stays with the person setting off the fireworks. And a fire crew will be on site. They even agreed to let kids climb on the truck earlier in the day."

Nolan's jaw tightened and he looked away.

"What's the real problem with the fireworks?" I asked.

"With all that's happened this summer, do you really want to risk more campers' safety with something like this? What if there's a fire or an explosion? What if debris falls on someone? I don't think this is a smart idea."

Heat flared up my neck and I took a step back. "Where is all this coming from? Mark is a professional. You were there when he looked at the lake a month ago to make sure there was enough room and that nothing would be in the way. If there is high wind or lightning, he won't do it. It's all in the contract, if you want to read it."

"Forget it." Nolan stalked off.

"What about this turtle?" I called after him.

He didn't turn back around.

I was distracted for a moment by the way his jeans cradled his butt, but my confusion and irritation over his crankiness quickly ruined it. Gar looked up at me as if to ask what Nolan's problem was.

I glanced back at the turtle, and she snapped her jaw in defiance.

"Do you have a problem with fireworks, too?"

She pulled her head into her shell.

"I guess everyone is grumpy today."

If Nolan wouldn't help, I knew I could count on my friend and local honey supplier, Hennie, and her skills with various wild creatures. I took my phone from my pocket and called, then left a message in her voicemail saying, "I need your help. We have a giant turtle and can't move it. Stop down when you finish your honey deliveries."

I then called Enid at Rollie's and explained, "I have a massive turtle in my driveway, and I'm not sure what to do about it."

"Well, dear, I can tell you, they are stubborn things. I couldn't get rid of old Speedy once he showed up. That diaper is the only concession I could get him to make."

"You didn't bring the turtle to the store?"

She laughed. "Goodness, no. He just got in one day and refused to leave. Pooped all over and made a dreadful mess. I was so glad when the diaper worked out. Though, it's not fun changing him. Worse than a baby."

I wrinkled my nose in disgust. "Do you think the turtle on my road will move on her own?"

"Well, she has to eat sometime, doesn't she?"

"Right." I sighed. "I guess I can put up a sign or something until she moves so she doesn't get run over. Thanks, Enid."

"Anytime, Thea. You and that cute boyfriend of yours stop by and see me soon."

"I told you, he's not my boyfriend. We're just keeping things casual."

"Sure, dear. Bye, bye now."

When I ended the call, I checked online to see how often alligator snapping turtles ate. Once every other day. Hopefully it'd been a while since her last meal.

Nolan was quiet most of the day, which still frustrated me. I didn't have time to do much about it because I was deep into Fourth of July planning. So many little things left to order or confirm: food, drinks, games, contests, crowd control. Every element needed to be perfect. And I still had to come in under budget somehow. The afternoon flew by without me taking a break from planning.

When Sally stuck her head in my office to say goodbye for the day, I rubbed my eyes and looked at the clock.

"Guess it's a good time for me to quit, too," I said.

Sally scrunched her face and played with her fingers. "Could I ask one little teensy favor?"

"Sure. What's up?"

"Well, if you could just not mention the turtle? Or not advertise it anywhere?"

I raised an eyebrow. "I hope she's gone when I walk outside. I don't want her sticking around, either. I thought your boys would be excited, though."

"Well, that's the thing. I've been thinking about it, and if they know there's a turtle here, they'll want to come with me to work to see it. And then they'll see the puppy and the kittens and remember the pool and the playground, and they won't ever want to leave. And I just... can't have that. They'll be running crazy while I'm trying to work and have a little quiet." She laughed nervously.

I thought for a moment, then got an idea. "The thing is, I can't really have kids running around while you're working, so you just tell them that your boss is mean and won't let them come with you."

Her face lit up. "That's perfect! Thank you!" She hugged her purse tight to her chest. "Maybe I can take some photos and that will be good enough."

"And hopefully the turtle will be long gone by the Fourth."

"Oh, right." Sally's face fell. "They'll be here for that, won't they?"

"That doesn't change the fact that you're not allowed to have them here while you're working." I made a fake stern face.

She nodded once, hard. "Right. That's all I have to say. Mommy's not allowed, and that's that." The grin returned, and she waved her fingers before walking out of sight.

Hearing stories about her four-year-old twin boys made me feel a rare moment of relief that I didn't have any kids of my own. Sally seemed to enjoy her job as registration person mostly because it got her out of the house and away from the chaos of her home life.

I stood to stretch and walked outside into the evening light. To my great relief, no turtle sat on the driveway. I moved the Stop sign back into its proper place in front of the gate.

I called to Nolan on the walkie, "I'm done for the night. Do you have my dog?"

"Yes. I also have burgers ready to grill. Want to eat?"

My late lunch had been rushed and was hours ago. "Be right there."

I walked past several occupied tent sites on my way to the seasonal section, where Nolan's site was. Many campers were cooking over fires, enjoying a quiet evening. I waved as I walked by, grateful for each one of them.

I reached Curtis's site, and his camper was bright inside with music pouring through the walls. For a moment, Curtis and his girlfriend, Rose, were visible through the window. Curtis held her close, and they danced in a slow, stiff shuffle. I smiled and chuckled to myself. Ever since Curtis had laid eyes on the widowed cornhole champion last month, he'd been smitten. And I suspected Rose was the reason Curtis continued to wear his decades-old Navy uniform to work, though it wasn't a requirement for his job surveilling the campground. It was nice to think that even at 82, love could be found.

When I neared Nolan's site, the farthest back from the rest of the campground, the smell of charcoal and cooking meat wafted from behind his camper. He'd built a small deck out back so he could sit facing the woods. I circled the camper, and Gar bounded over to me, licking my hand in greeting.

"Smells good," I said.

Nolan stood behind the grill, arms crossed, watching the burgers sizzle. I barely received a glance and a head nod for a hello.

I sat in one of his padded folding chairs and leaned back, looking up into the darkening sky as the stars blinked into view. Crickets sang as the grill popped and hissed. I took in several long breaths and tried to figure out what I failed to see in the situation. What bothered Nolan so deeply?

By the time the burgers were ready, he still hadn't said a word. He handed me a plate and sat in the chair beside mine, then stuffed his burger into his mouth. I did the same. He wouldn't be much good for talking while he ate, anyhow.

We finished the burgers—one for me, three for him—and he sat up in his chair, tapping his fingertips together.

"What are you waiting for?" My voice sounded thunderous as it broke the silent tension between us.

"What do you mean?" He didn't look at me.

"There's obviously something going on with you, but you haven't said what."

He growled and rubbed his forehead.

I watched him for several long minutes. "Nolan, please."

He huffed. "Look. If there will be fireworks on the Fourth, I can't be here."

"I don't get it. What's the big deal?"

"It's not so much the fireworks themselves as the sounds they make."

I considered his words, but things weren't adding up. "Do you have sensitive ears?"

He shook his head. "You know it's common for soldiers to get PTSD, right?"

"I don't see how you couldn't."

He shrugged. "Some things are more common triggers than others."

"And the fireworks... remind you of war?"

"They sound like gunfire and bombs. It's worse when it's unexpected. So, if you're going to allow campers to set them off, even those little snapping ones..."

I hadn't considered something like that. I suffered from PTSD myself, so I understood how triggers worked, but mine were very different from what Nolan experienced. Loud, sudden noises rarely bothered me.

"I'm sorry. I didn't realize," I said. "We don't have to allow campers to have them. That sounds dangerous, anyhow."

"I usually retreat into the woods for several days this time of year to escape it. Don't know what I'll do this year."

"I didn't mean to create a difficult situation for you."

"It's fine. I'll figure something out. But you might need extra security if I have to be gone."

"Sure." I nodded. "I certainly won't make you stay somewhere that might upset you or make you feel unsafe."

He looked at me sideways. "Don't do that."

"What am I doing?"

"Acting like I'm some kind of pansy for not wanting to be around fireworks."

"I didn't say anything like that," I snapped.

He rubbed the back of his neck and chugged a beer that had been sitting by his foot. He crumpled the can and threw it across the deck. "People who haven't been there don't understand. It's not like I'm *afraid* of loud noises."

I pulled in a slow breath and tried to decide how to respond. His anger spiked my anxiety. "Nolan, you're the toughest, strongest, manliest man I've ever known. I doubt you're afraid of anything. But I can understand a little. I mean, when goofing around almost gives you a panic attack, it's not much fun, either."

It had been a day not long after I hired Nolan that we'd been playing around with the hose and he'd grabbed me in a bear hug. It still made my heart pound to think of the feeling of being held against my will, unable to break free. I reached over and put my hand on his.

"If I thought you were any kind of pansy," I continued, "I wouldn't pay you to do security, and I definitely wouldn't call you every time something scary happens."

After several minutes, he turned to me. "Want to go for a walk?"

I nodded and stood. He held my hand as we circled around the looping roads of the campground with Gar in tow. Nolan didn't say much and neither did I. The few times I'd seen him rattled by something, he tended to be quiet. Lost in his own thoughts, hopefully not beating himself up too much.

We strolled along every road, not in any hurry. By the time we ended up near the path to my cabin, it had been an hour. The kittens ran in front of us as we turned down the trail. Three sets of black paw prints dotted the path. "I can only imagine what those three get up to all day."

Nolan walked me to my door and gave me a long kiss goodnight. The relief from his affection melted over me and filled my chest with warmth. He squeezed my hands before turning away.

"Hey," I said.

He paused and looked over his shoulder.

"Don't stress over this."

He nodded and walked off.

I let Gar inside and poured food into his bowl. While he chomped it down, I leaned my elbows on the kitchen counter and thought through what Nolan had said and not said.

How many others were like him, dreading this holiday? What if somehow I could make Cedar Fish safe for Nolan, but also for anyone who might want to escape the noise and still enjoy the Fourth? Nolan never talked about being a soldier or the aftereffects of it. I wished I knew more about his time in the military and as a cop and what things still haunted him from those days. I also still didn't know why he'd been fired from the force, and anytime I asked, he changed the subject. Something deep in my soul worried it might be so bad that if I knew, I'd change my mind about him.

I considered Nolan's pained expression, his hesitation at even admitting something was bothering him. My chest ached for him. There was only one thing to do. I'd have to cancel the fireworks display. The deposit money would be gone, but I'd get back my first payment, according to the contract. The idea of losing that money sat like a rock in my stomach, but what choice did I have? I just hoped I had time to rebrand the event and bring in enough reservations to make up for the money I'd lose on the fireworks.

CHAPTER 2

I had put off calling Mark Dorsey for most of the morning. The later it got, the more I dreaded it. But it was time to get it over with.

I closed the door to my office and picked up the phone to dial.

He answered, "Dorsey Fireworks."

"Hi Mark, this is Thea Pagoni from Cedar Fish Campground."

"Hey there. What can I do for you?"

I sucked in a breath. "I'm afraid that I need to cancel my contract."

"Cancel? What do you mean?"

"We're going to make this a quiet event, safe for vets."

"Safe for vets? What in the—? I'll have you know, I am a veteran of the Vietnam War, and I find fireworks perfectly safe. I don't put on a dangerous display, Miss Pagoni."

"It's not that. Not dangerous. Some vets find the noise to be triggering."

"The noise? That doesn't make much sense."

I let out a heavy sigh. "Then I assume you don't suffer from PTSD, Mr. Dorsey. But many do, and I want to honor our vets with a safe, noise-controlled event."

"Do you think I don't honor my fellow vets? You think I'm doing something wrong here?"

"That's not what I'm saying at all." I stood up and paced. "You put on a certain type of show, and it's perfect for many people. Most people love fireworks. Just not all people, and those are the people I want to serve with my event."

"It's only a week and a half until the fourth! Anyone wanting a display has already booked someone. I'll never be able to get a new contract in time!"

"I'm sorry about that. I really am. If I had known sooner—"

"Well, sorry doesn't get me a booking on the busiest day of the year. You're taking a prime opportunity from me! I can't make this much money any other day of the year!"

I gritted my teeth and steadied myself. "I understand that you're upset, and again, I apologize. The contract does allow me to cancel up to seven days before the event for a refund minus the deposit. And we're nine days out. It's your contract, not mine."

"Oh, so you're a lawyer now, are you? Ha. You're nothing but a flighty woman who can't make up her damn mind."

"Excuse me?" Anger flared up my neck and I gripped my phone harder. "I'll have you know that I am a lawyer, actually. And I don't appreciate you calling me names. This is business. Sometimes it sucks and you lose money. Get over it."

I ended the call and slammed my phone down. My entire body shook.

I picked my phone back up and dialed again. This time, a nice young woman answered the phone, and I tried to remove the rage from my voice.

"Hello. I need to stop payment on a check." No way would I trust Mark to give me back the payment he'd walked out with.

When I was through with my call to the bank, I stormed out of my office and headed down the smaller loop of tent sites. I found Gar sniffing around outside of the bathroom. He ran over to greet me, then returned to his exploration. Inside the bathroom, Nolan twisted a wrench around a pipe. His pants and shirt were more wet than dry.

"Is it going okay?" I asked.

"Yup. Plumbing is just messy. What's up?"

"I want you to keep an eye out for Mark Dorsey."

He paused to look at me. "Why?"

"I called to cancel the contract, and he didn't take it well. He insulted me, and I'm not sure what will happen if he brings my check back."

Nolan set the wrench down and faced me. "You cancelled the contract?"

I nodded. "I don't want to make you uncomfortable, and I thought it would be a good opportunity to provide a safe place for other vets who might feel the same way about fireworks."

He blinked at me. "You're changing the whole event?"

"Well, not the whole event. Most things will be the same, but I am going to ban any sort of fireworks or noisemakers, and I thought we might do some sort of video display on a screen with music instead of explosions."

"You cancelled the fireworks for me?"

"Not *only* for you." I tilted my head and gave him a sheepish grin. "I guess that means I like you or something."

He pulled me into a one-armed hug and gave me a quick kiss. "That makes my Fourth a whole lot better."

"There is one small condition."

He raised an eyebrow at me.

"I need your help. I don't know much about this. I Googled some, but, you know, that only tells you so much. I'm not sure how else to make this a good event for vets."

"Not much to know. Food, good. Music, good. No loud, sudden sounds, good."

I tapped my lips. "What about Hennie? She's up there shooting all the time at her cabin. Has that ever been a problem?"

He shook his head. "Far enough away."

"Good. Then, if you have any other ideas, let me know. In the meantime, I'll figure out how to rebrand this thing and target our new demographic."

"I'll get the word out with some friends back in St. Louis. I think I could get a few to come."

"Perfect. I'm headed back to work. I'll leave Gar out here with you so he's not stuck inside all day."

Nolan nodded and watched me with a smile on his face. I petted Gar goodbye and returned to my office.

I worked for a few minutes on the new flyers, until Sally knocked on my door.

"Come in," I told her.

Sally stuck her head in and whispered, "Someone here to see you."

I gulped and stood up. "Is it Mark Dorsey?"

"No. It's a woman I don't know."

Maybe it was all right then. I braved a peek into the main office and didn't recognize the person at the counter. I let out a breath. "Thanks."

Sally looked back, then whispered, "It's a *sales* call. Should I get rid of her?"

"No, that's okay." I hadn't interacted much with other local business owners, and networking a little never hurt.

I walked out to meet the woman who wore a blond ponytail and a bubblegum pink pencil skirt under a crisp white polo shirt. She looked out of place in our dusty office store. Then I noticed the white box in her hands, and my curiosity grew.

"Can I help you?"

"Hello there." She gave a sunny smile, and her hand shot out to me. "I'm Kimberly Henson, owner of Kimmy Cakes."

I shook her hand, her extreme perkiness not sitting well on top of my residual anger. "Thea Pagoni. What can I do for you?"

"I'd like to offer you some sample muffins. They're delicious, baked fresh, and I deliver. I think Kimmy Cakes products would be a fabulous addition to the other products in your store."

I glanced behind her to the display of sunscreen and bug spray, the bags of marshmallows stuffed beside the boxes of graham crackers and Hershey bars. We sold tons of ice cream, bottled drinks, and s'mores and hotdog fixings, but we didn't have much selection in the way of food. Certainly nothing that wasn't boxed, bagged, or jarred. My plans for converting part of the rec hall into a snack bar were a distant dream.

"Thanks for stopping by," I said. "But I don't really think baked goods are the sort of thing my campers are looking for."

"Just wait until you try one. Sure to change your mind every time." Kimberly opened the box and took out a large blueberry muffin topped with crystals of sugar.

"It looks good, but I'm not in the position to be adding new products."

"Did you notice the festive wrapper?" She balanced the muffin on her palm so I could see the red and blue fireworks.

"We're actually having a sound-safe Fourth of July here. No fireworks. Thanks anyway."

"Maybe you could just try one tiny little bite?"

My jaw clenched, and I tried not to unleash on her. I didn't want to see her mascara run. I picked up the muffin, pulled down one side of the wrapper and took a bite. It was moist, sweet, and full of blueberry. Not a bad muffin. Still not an ideal product.

"They're very good. Why don't you leave a card, and if we ever need anything, I'll give you a call."

"Oh, sure! I make festive cupcakes, too." She grinned and pointed at me. "No fireworks, though, of course."

"Cupcakes might be a good idea for our event, actually."

"In that case, I'll leave you this." She slid a price sheet across the counter, then picked up another muffin and held it out to Sally. "Would you like a sample, too?"

Sally looked surprised but smiled and accepted the muffin. "Thank you. I'm on a diet and can't have sugar, but my boys will love this."

"Kids!" Kimberly clapped and grinned. "I love to do kids' cakes and cookies. I'll give you a flyer for our birthday parties. Any flavor you can imagine, I can bake it."

Kimberly handed Sally a colorful flyer and turned back to me. "Is your event on the fourth?"

"It is."

"I still have a few spots available for orders, but they're filling up fast, so let me know." She stuck her hand out again. "So great to meet you!"

"You, too. Thanks."

Kimberly left the office, and the whole store seemed to dim.

"She was awful cheery, wasn't she?" I said to Sally.

"Mm hmm." Sally nodded enthusiastically while studying the flyer. "These cakes are really cute."

"I think I might give her a try for our event. Cupcakes would be a nice addition."

Sally set the muffin under the counter beside her purse. "That'll keep the boys up late, for sure." She chewed her fingernail and stared hard at a spot of dirt on the floor.

"You don't have to give it to them, you know."

She let out an awkward, high-pitched giggle and waved me off. "I know."

Before I could say more, a camper entered the store. He stood in the personal-care aisle, looking over the lotions carefully.

"Can I help you find anything?" I asked.

Behind me, Sally gasped. I spun to see her eyes wide and mouth hanging open. Her hands waved frantically around her face, and she hopped from foot to foot, mouthing, "Oh, my gosh. Oh, my gosh. Oh, my gosh."

"What's wrong?"

"That's Jerry Bishop!" she whispered and grabbed my arm as she watched the camper.

Jerry picked up a bottle of sunscreen, read the label, then set it back down and chose a different bottle. He wore simple khaki shorts and a pale-blue short-sleeved button-down shirt. The baseball cap on his head was plain black—no logos, no slogans. His sneakers were an expensive brand, but looked neither crisp white nor trashed and falling apart. I couldn't get a good read on what type of person he was.

"Do you know him?" I asked Sally quietly.

"Don't you?" She blinked at me with shock in her round eyes.

I shook my head.

"He's the designer of Bishop Purses!"

"Oh," I said. "I'm not really into handbags." I owned a few and had carried one every day in my former career as a lawyer, but the campground life provided less occasion. The one purse I kept came from a department store and was no brand name worth noting.

"Well, he is *the* most sought-after designer in all of Outer Branson. You have to get on a waiting list just to see his purses when he opens a sale. Then there's a lottery to decide who gets to buy them. They cost thousands of dollars."

I looked again at Jerry. I guessed his clothing was pricey, but aside from the professional business attire I'd worn in my lawyer days, I didn't have much experience with high-end brands. His overwhelmingly average appearance didn't give me the impression of some wealthy fashion designer. He was still inspecting the bottles of sunscreen like it was the biggest purchase he would make that month.

"Thousands?" I asked.

Sally nodded hard enough to make her shoulder-length waves bounce. "I am *so* excited!" She clapped her hands together and squealed quietly, then whispered, "I *finally* made it into the lottery. For years, I was stuck on the waiting list—until last month. This is my big chance to win a slot to buy a purse! The lottery is only a few days away. This has to be a sign, Jerry showing up here like this. I just know it!"

I looked again at Jerry Bishop, famous purse designer. The thing that stood out most about him was his strange behavior. Maybe that added to his mystique? He seemed to be having trouble deciding on sunscreen.

I asked him, "Did you need help finding anything?"

"Is this the only brand of sunscreen you have?" Jerry faced the bottle toward me.

"Yes."

He set it down and picked up a spray can. "And this bug spray? Is this the only type you have?"

"Yes."

He read the back of the bug spray before setting it down and picking up the sunscreen again.

I whispered to Sally, "You sure this guy is a purse designer?"

She nodded enthusiastically, her eyes still wide and starry. "Only the best designer ever."

"How about goat repellant?" Jerry asked. "Do you carry goat repellant?"

I blinked at him. "I didn't even know that was a thing."

"How else would you keep goats away?"

"Uhh..." I lifted my hands. "Ours here are pretty gentle, so I don't think you'll need repellant. And they're behind the fence, so they can't attack you or anything."

Jerry looked at me, took in my words, and set the bug spray back down. "Oh, do you sell muffins?" He pointed to the partially eaten blueberry muffin, still sitting on the counter near the cash register.

"No. That was just a sample."

I couldn't tell if my answers were disappointing him or not. Sally hung on his every word and inched closer and closer to the counter.

"Can I get some change for the feed machine?" Jerry took his wallet out.

"You want to help him?" I whispered to Sally.

She sucked in a breath and shook her head, backing away. "I couldn't possibly."

Jerry handed me a dollar, and I opened the drawer to give him four quarters.

"That reminds me." He left the quarters on the counter and turned to walk down an aisle. He picked up a small bottle of hand sanitizer and read the label. When he turned to face me, I guessed what was coming.

"It's the only kind we have," I said.

He nodded and set the bottle back down. Then he walked into the first aisle, picked up the sunscreen and bug spray again, and carried them to the counter.

I rang up his items, but before I could give him a total, he darted away. He picked up the hand sanitizer and brought it over to join his other items.

"That everything?" I asked.

He nodded.

I added the hand sanitizer and gave him the total.

"Oh, wait." He went into another aisle and came back several minutes later with a pack of gum. He held it up. "Is this—"

"The only brand we have. You saw the different flavors?"

"I only chew peppermint."

"Then that's the only one."

He set it on the counter with the other items.

"That everything?"

He nodded again.

I gave him his new total and held my breath, expecting him to add something else. Instead, he opened his wallet and handed me a twenty. I gave him his change and put his items into a plastic bag. He didn't say a word as he walked outside.

When the door closed behind him, Sally let out a long sigh and sank onto the counter like a lovesick teenager.

"He must make some beautiful purses," I said.

"They're amazing." Sally took out her phone and tapped several times, then held the screen so I could see a collection of Bishops.

I squinted at them and looked more closely. "Are they all... triangular?"

Sally bobbed her head. "That's how you know it's a Bishop. It's his signature shape."

I nodded slowly. I'd never seen a triangular purse before, nor did they seem particularly functional to me. What happened when you set it down? And that point at the bottom seemed like a deadly trap for junk gathering.

I shrugged. "I guess people have all different tastes."

Sally huffed and put a hand on her hip. "Well, he's won lots of awards."

"I guess I don't really know purses."

She put her hand to her mouth and giggled. "Can I tell you a secret?"

"Sure."

She leaned closer and whispered, "Part of the reason I took this job was to save up to buy one. When I made it into the lottery, my husband agreed to let me buy one if I won, but we don't have the money for it, so here I am."

"Huh. Well, good luck. I hope you can... win your right to buy a very expensive"—and downright ugly, I thought—"purse."

"Thank you." She put her hand to her heart and sighed toward the door. "Wait until I tell my friends that Jerry Bishop is staying here!"

She took out her phone again, and I disappeared into my office.

CHAPTER 3

I worked uninterrupted for an entire ten minutes before Sally called my name again. When I walked back into the main office, she stood nervously in front of a woman who looked angry and unfamiliar to me. *Oh, great.* I loved taking customer complaints.

"Hi there," I said. I started to rethink my initial assumption. Most of our campers did not wear bright pink skirt suits with big, chunky necklaces. This woman's tall hair would catch on fire from all the product she used if she tried to roast a hot dog, and her cloud of perfume would attract swarms of mosquitos. She couldn't be an angry camper, after all.

"Are you Thea Pagoni?" the woman demanded.

"Yes." I put my hand on Sally's shoulder and told her, "Thanks."

She gave a grateful smile and moved away from us, toward the reservation book.

"What can I do for you?" I asked.

The woman put one hand on her hip and jutted her chin out. "I'm Linda Dorsey. Mark Dorsey's wife?"

I pulled in a sharp breath and my stomach tightened.

"I came to talk to you about your fireworks display."

"What about it?" I said bravely. "I cancelled it. In fact, I was just working on the flyer advertising it as a sound-safe event for vets."

Linda let out a high-pitched laugh. "Don't you know that vets *love* fireworks? You know those USO shows? Tons of fireworks, and the men love them." She leaned in conspiratorially. "Well, that and the women in skimpy clothes." She winked.

"I'm sure many do. But not all. Look, I already explained this to your husband—"

"No, let me explain this to *you*. You can't cancel! Don't you know what that means for us?"

"Umm... that you can book another event and charge extra for the short notice?"

She narrowed her eyes. "People don't book things like a fireworks display last minute. There are permits and things that have to be done ahead of time. Which you know, because you've already done all the hard work."

I nodded. "I realize that, but it was a decision that had to be made."

"Well, *unmake* it," she said through gritted teeth. "We can't lose this money! We need your booking. Please." The whiney tone in her voice made me squirm.

"I'm sorry. I know it puts you in a bad position, but I'm within my rights, according to the contract."

"The contract!" She tossed her hands into the air. "The contract is for indecent people. You're not an indecent person, are you?" She batted her clumpy eyelashes at me.

"I try not to be."

"Then it's all settled. You'll go ahead and rebook and that's that."

I pressed my palms flat on the counter and wished I had my ice to chomp on. "I will not be rebooking. I'm sorry. Now—"

"No!" Linda stomped her high-heeled foot and crossed her arms.

I stepped back. I glanced over my shoulder to Sally, who held the walkie talkie in her hand, ready to call security.

"You see, the thing is—" Linda set her purse on the counter. The triangular shape made it fall over as she dug inside it. I almost rolled my eyes at the gaudy orange leather fringe and brass fixtures. Must be one of those "amazing" Bishop purses.

"Where *is* it?" Linda hissed. The more she dug, the more panicky I grew. For a moment, I thought she might pull out a gun or a knife. I took another step backward.

Linda pulled out a round, white candy. Several clear cellophane wrappers tumbled onto the counter. Each was stamped with the green Mint-Os logo.

Linda popped the mint into her mouth. "If you cancel your event, I have to cancel my vacation. And I could really, really use a vacation."

I swept the candy wrappers into my hand and turned to throw them in the trashcan behind me, not hiding my irritated glare. "I'm sorry to hear that," I said. "I really am. I'm sure you deserve a vacation and would enjoy spending quality time with your husband."

She huffed and waved me off. "I said I need a vacation, not a headache. We spend our traveling time mostly apart. Otherwise, I have to listen to him ramble on and on about chemicals and explosions and things I don't care about. But, on vacation, I can go to the spa to get a massage and get my hair and nails done." She patted the sides of her tall hair. Her nails were at least a half-inch past her fingers and covered in bright-pink, glittery polish.

"Again, I'm sorry. But I can't change the event just because of your vacation."

"But you changed your event because the vets don't like it."

I had come to the end of what I could tolerate before I turned inappropriately snippy. "I'm sorry again, Linda. I am. But, if you'll excuse me, I have a phone call to make." I turned to walk away.

"You'll be sorry!"

I glanced back as she zipped her purse up and slung it over her shoulder. Then she spun and stormed out, slamming the door behind her.

I looked at Sally, who chewed on her lip nervously.

"That was fun," I said.

The door immediately opened again, and I balled my hands, ready to fight Linda off if it came to that. I felt relieved to see Jerry instead. My relief ended when he opened his mouth.

"That feed machine." He pointed toward the wildlife area. "Is that the only type of feed you sell?"

I pulled in a deep breath before answering, "Yes."

"Oh. Then I guess I need more quarters." He took out another dollar and handed it to me.

Before I opened the drawer, I asked, "Did you need anything else?"

"Just the quarters."

"You're sure?"

He nodded.

I gave him the change and closed the drawer.

"Do you have any sort of goat call?" he asked.

Was he serious? "A goat call?"

"To make them come to you. I'm trying to feed them, but they won't all come."

Hadn't he been asking about goat *repellant* earlier? "Some goats are more aggressive than others," I explained.

"So, you don't have any sort of goat call, then?"

"Nope."

"How about one for deer?"

"I think that's something only hunters use," I said.

"But do you have any of them here?"

"No."

"And is that the only wildlife area you have?"

I nodded. "There's wildlife all around us, but we only have the one enclosed area. I guess we have one of lots of things." Like the one nerve I had left to deal with him.

"Well, you have more than one goat, but I can't seem to feed any except the one!" He shook his head.

"They all get fed regularly, so don't worry."

"If I buy a cup of feed, I want to feed all the goats, not only *some* of the goats."

"I understand," I lied. "But unfortunately, I don't think the goats will."

"I'll try buying more feed and see if I can get the others to come on out."

"I hope that works."

Jerry picked up his quarters and left.

I looked at my watch. Close enough. "I'm stepping out for lunch before any other crazy customers or vendors can come in."

Sally clutched the walkie talkie to her chest. "I'll just give you a call if anyone else needs you."

I pressed my lips into a line. "You do that."

Outside, I took in deep lungfuls of the smooth wilderness air. Today was unusually cool for June, and the humidity hadn't yet spiked. It would be a good day to go for a run. If I was into that sort of thing.

I took out my phone and texted Nolan. "You busy? I need a lunch break."

He responded, "Perfect timing. Was just putting together a sandwich for me and Gar."

"You're feeding Gar a sandwich?"

He sent back a smiley face. I rolled my eyes and took the first right toward Nolan's camper. When I reached his site, the door was open and Gar sat outside, chewing a bone. When I looked closer at his snack, I saw it was two dog biscuits with what I thought was peanut butter between them. Gar was so engrossed in his meal, he lifted his head when I petted him, but didn't get up to greet me.

I stepped up two metal stairs into Nolan's camper. "Nice doggie sandwich."

"A little peanut butter for him, a little peanut butter for me. And you, too. You want one?"

Nolan stood at his small square of a kitchen counter, pieces of bread stacked high beside jars of grape jelly and peanut butter. Crumbs covered the space and congregated on a sticky pocketknife with its blade extended.

"Are you... using your pocketknife to spread the peanut butter and jelly?"

He picked up the knife. "It's great for so many things. Always gotta have a knife on you."

"What happened to your silverware?"

He jerked his thumb toward the tiny sink. Dishes towered high enough to block the faucet from view.

"Maybe invest in some disposables?"

"Why? I got what I need right here." He patted the knife, slapped together two slathered pieces of bread, and handed me the sandwich.

I took a bite and jelly squished out, dripping onto the floor. "It's obvious I need to cook for you more."

He glanced at the jelly and whistled. Gar bounced inside, shaking the camper with his weight. He looked to Nolan, who pointed to the spot. Gar licked up the jelly, came to me to get petted, then leapt back outside.

"I'm thinking maybe Gar should stay with me more, even if he is stuck inside all day. What other bad habits have you taught him?"

Nolan balanced a stack of sandwiches in one hand and grabbed a bag of chips with the other. I followed him out to his back porch, where we sat in the reclining folding chairs to eat.

"I came up with a catchphrase for the event," I told him between bites. "A 'sound-safe' event."

"I like it." He finished his first sandwich in three bites and went for the next. "I talked to a few friends and there are a few more I plan to reach out to."

"Perfect. And if you know of any organizations we can contact to have them post our flyers, let me know."

"The VA hospital would be good. And there's a legion in town that would post a flyer."

"There is? I wouldn't have even known that." I pulled my mini notebook from my pocket and flipped a few pages. "What about renting one of those big, inflatable screens to show a fireworks display? And then some speakers for the music."

"That would be cool. Ever consider a local band? I hear there are a few decent ones around."

"That's a good idea." I noted it. "I was thinking about a contest for our campers. Something like the best decorated campsite wins a free weekend of camping."

He nodded and chewed. "That's fun."

We continued to brainstorm while we ate. By the time we finished, I had several new ideas and felt refreshed. Taking a break to event plan with Nolan was exactly what I had needed.

"I better get back." I stood to stretch. "With the morning I had, who knows what the afternoon will hold."

He gave me a quick, sticky kiss, and I looked over at Gar, considering. He bounded around the campsite, stopped to sniff a flower, then jumped away from it and ran to stand at attention as a camper walked by. When the camper passed, Gar returned to his exploration. He looked like he was having fun. Much more fun than he would sitting inside the office with me. I decided to leave him to it and walked back to the office alone.

When I entered, I asked Sally, "Everything been okay while I was at lunch?"

"Oh, sure. Had a few checking in, one checked out, and I took a new reservation." She pointed to the entry in the book.

I still hadn't addressed our paper reservation system, though it was one of the first things I thought needed to change when I took the campground over.

"How are you with computers?" I asked.

"Well, I used them some at school, but that's been over ten years."

"I've been meaning to switch us over to a digital reservation system. I think it'll be much easier."

She let out a huge sigh. "Good. The logbook is so confusing! If things aren't written down the same way each time, sometimes the information I need isn't there, and having those forms just gets to be too much."

"Glad you're onboard with the change." Now I just had to research software options and find one that was easy enough to use, cost effective, and designed to fit our needs. Maybe after the Fourth of July event was set, I'd focus on that project.

The office door opened, and I looked up to see Jerry walk in again. I steadied myself for his barrage of questions.

He walked to the drink cooler and selected a bottle of water, then brought it to the counter. I hesitated. When he didn't ask if we had any other water available, I grew curious.

"Anything else?" I entered the water's price, but didn't total the transaction yet.

He shook his head.

I gave him his total, but noticed he looked a little pale. Jerry was also sweating a lot—much more than the cool day called for. "Are you feeling okay?"

He wiped his forehead. "I'm going to head back to my tent to rest, but I want to finish feeding the goats first." He seemed to wobble a little on his feet.

"Are you sure? Maybe it would be better to finish later. You look like you might pass out."

"I still have feed left." He looked at me like this should have been an obvious explanation for why he was risking his health and safety.

"Well, just let me know if you need anything."

When he left, I picked up the walkie. "Hey Curtis, where are you?"

There was a long pause, then a muffled, "Yes, Miss Thea?" I heard giggling in the background and knew he must be with Rose.

"Could you keep an eye on the guy at the wildlife area? He's looking a little ill."

"Yes, ma'am."

I turned to Sally. "If you don't need anything, I'm going to research local bands. Do you know any?"

"Oh, sure! There's the Little Blue Band, the Woopiloos..." She scrunched her face in thought. "Oh! Trumpet Sam! The kids love him."

"I was thinking something a little more adult."

"Oh." She blew out a breath. "I wouldn't know anything about those bands."

In my office, I started with social media. When I searched "Outer Branson bands," several profiles came up. I watched a few videos and wrote down some decent options. I'd have Nolan listen to them later and help me decide.

I reviewed my numbers from our Memorial Day event to figure out how many cupcakes I'd be looking at. Probably a few hundred would be eaten. Before I could call Kimmy Cakes, I heard a commotion in the main office and hurried out to see what was going on. A group of campers all spoke at the same time to a confused and flustered Sally.

The three thirty-something men looked terrified. Their hands waved in the air and pointed. I blinked at them and tried to sort out what they were saying. One pointed toward the door and said loudly to me, "There's a dead body in the goat pen!"

"Do you mean a dead goat or a...?" I bit my lip, hoping.

They shook their heads. "It's a man."

I swallowed and slowly reached for the walkie talkie. "Nolan?"

"What's up?" he answered.

I felt as if I had left my body and floated above it. Not a third death. It wasn't possible. I squeezed the walkie button until my knuckles turned white. "I— We— The goats..."

"I'm on my way."

CHAPTER 4

I met Nolan outside at the wildlife pen as Curtis and Rose pulled up in the golf cart. The ducks were busy swimming in the pond, and the deer hid in the small shelter in the center of the area. Gar ran along the fence, chasing and disturbing the chickens. Jerry's body lay facedown near the fence, a goat standing nearby to keep guard. I had to look away as my stomach tightened.

"I don't think he's doing real well," Curtis hollered.

"No, I'd say not." I gave Nolan a pleading look. "This can't be happening again."

He pressed his lips into a line. "Let's make sure he's really dead."

"What?" I shrieked. "How? You can't touch him!"

"Thea, a man collapsed on the grounds. The first thing we should do is call an ambulance and give him CPR."

"I'll call an ambulance then." I took out my phone and dialed, keeping my distance as Nolan approached the body.

He hopped over the fence and shoved the goat away before carefully turning Jerry over. He put his head near Jerry's face. I called Gar to me and had him sit. The animals didn't need to be any more riled up than they already were.

The dispatcher answered, "What's your emergency?"

"Hi, this is Thea Pagoni from Cedar Fish Campground. We've had a man collapse and..."

Nolan looked at me and shook his head.

"And he's not breathing," I added.

"Does he have a pulse?" the dispatcher asked.

Nolan held his fingertips to Jerry's wrist a moment, then shook his head again.

"No, he doesn't have a pulse." As I said the words, I stumbled backward in the grass. My ears rang and black spotted my vision. I sat hard and didn't register the sound of Hennie's four-wheeler until it stopped right in front of me.

The dispatcher gave directions for CPR, but Nolan was already at work doing chest compressions.

Hennie hopped off her four-wheeler, her tall galoshes squishing in the grass. Her long, silvery hair was in its usual braid, trailing down her short-sleeved button-down work shirt. "Oh man, what'd I miss? Sorry I didn't make it down yesterday. Had an issue with one of my honey deliveries. Does this have anything to do with the turtle?"

I shook my head and couldn't say more. Hennie wandered over toward Nolan, and I focused back on the dispatcher.

"The ambulance is on the way, but it may still be a few minutes."

"Thank you," I said absently as I ended the call.

Hennie came to pull me to my feet. "Looks like we got another murder to solve!"

"No, no." I waved my hands and shook my head. "This guy was sick. I saw him. He was all sweaty and pale."

"You always think it's an accident, and it always turns out to be a murder."

"This time it's really not a murder." I faced away from the pen but with Nolan visible in the corner of my eye. He knelt in front of Jerry, still doing compressions.

After many minutes, Nolan stopped and breathed out a sigh. "Man, this gets tiring."

"If he hasn't been breathing or had a pulse this long, I don't think you'll get him back," I said.

"He's getting stiff already!" Hennie pointed.

I dared to glance at the body and saw Jerry's hand raised a few inches off the ground.

Sweat ran down Nolan's face, but he resumed compressions for another few minutes. When he stopped, he shook out his arms and looked to me. "Do you think you can take over for a while?"

My eyes grew five sizes bigger, and the world tilted as I considered putting my hands on a dead body. I pressed my legs against Gar and dug my fingers into his hair to steady myself.

"Hennie?" Nolan gave her a hopeful look.

She cracked her knuckles and hopped inside the pen. "I'll give him a go."

Nolan stood beside me as Hennie got to work. Curtis stood beside the fence with his hands on his hips. Rose sat in the golf cart. She looked as freaked out as I felt.

"Curtis said you called him because the guy was sick?" Nolan asked.

I nodded. "I asked him to keep an eye on Jerry. Guess he was too late."

Curtis cleared his throat. "I was on my way, but was unexpectedly detained." He broke into a slow, toothy grin. His dentures slipped, and he sucked them back into place.

Was Rose's presence causing too much of a distraction? Curtis was a better problem to think about than Jerry lying dead with the goats, so I focused on that. Should I impose some restrictions on them? Like, no making out while on the clock?

Nolan interrupted my thoughts. "Unless the guy was poisoned, I think we're safe on this one."

"Poisoned? Why would you say that?" Panic exploded in my chest as I considered what that would mean.

"That seems to be how our luck goes around here," Nolan said. "I think we should take photos and make some notes just in case."

Hennie looked over at us and said, "Maybe you can advertise as the world's most haunted campground. I bet at Halloween time, we could make some haunted houses and get a ton of people walking through."

"Hennie." I shook my head at her. "It's almost the Fourth of July. We need the reservations from the rest of this season to even have another season. I can't be worried about Halloween now!"

"I'm just saying, is all. Look on the bright side."

"There is no bright side. A man is dead. We have another death in the campground."

Hennie stopped the compressions and looked at Nolan. "I guess there's no use in continuing CPR."

Nolan sighed. "Guess not." He jumped back in the pen and took photos. When he was done, he returned to my side. "I don't see any signs of injury. So, it wasn't like he fell in and broke his neck or anything."

"Well, good. That should limit our liability," I said. "One less thing to worry about. We need to see who he was camping with and notify them."

"Huh. That's odd." Nolan quirked an eyebrow. "Jerry's shorts... Have been eaten."

I tried to understand what he meant. I had to brave my first full look at the body to see for myself. Part of Jerry's khaki shorts was gone. Luckily, all of his private areas were still covered, but a chunk was missing where the pocket once was.

"What could have...?"

"The goat." Hennie pointed.

The goat that had been standing closest to Jerry was chewing. And chewing and chewing. A long, tan thread hung from his mouth.

"Are you telling me that the goat ate his shorts?"

Nolan shrugged. "Looks that way."

I asked Hennie, "Why would it do that? Will that hurt the goat?"

Hennie laughed. "Goats eat anything. Got the strongest stomachs around. He'll be just fine."

"Could the goat have done anything to Jerry?" I asked. "Is he responsible in any way?"

"Police don't usually have animals of interest," Nolan assured me.

"The police." I groaned. I thought I was through dealing with Officers Longshore and Randall. But now they'd be back, trying to figure out another death and still not having a clue.

Hennie had her eyes trained on the goat. "You know, I could get him to throw it up. Might be better for the goat, and we could make sure he didn't eat any evidence."

"Evidence? We don't need evidence this time," I insisted. "This time, it really isn't a murder."

"There's going to be evidence pointing to the cause of death, even if it's accidental," Nolan said. "In a case like this, I'd say they'll call in all sorts of people to take a look—ME, coroner, possibly a detective."

Tears welled up in my eyes. "I can't do this again. Why do people keep dying here?"

Nolan folded me into a hug. I let my forehead rest on his shoulder and breathed in his scent. Though he'd been working hard and was sweaty, he still smelled like his deodorant—a strong, spicy scent I found comfortingly familiar.

"The police will be here soon, and they'll get it all sorted out." He rubbed my back.

Hennie retrieved a rope from her four-wheeler, and I wondered if she had brought it along to do something about the turtle. Maybe she had planned to tow it off the road?

She jumped back in the pen and wrangled the goat. Once he was on his side, she tied the goat's legs up, then shoved her fingers down his throat. I turned away as the goat made a retching sound and threw up.

"That Hennie does come in handy," Nolan said.

"Well, lookey here!" Hennie stood and held out her hand.

Whatever she held dripped on the ground. I gagged and looked away.

"Oh, it's just a little goat spit up." She rolled her eyes and came closer. "This must've been what he was after." She held a wadded ball between her thumb and forefinger.

"What is it?" Nolan leaned in to inspect it.

"A wrapper of some sort," Hennie said.

I made myself look more closely at the crumpled ball. It did appear to be some kind of waxy paper, like that of a muffin or cupcake wrapper. I could just make out round, blue-purple stains that must've been from blueberries. "That was in Jerry's pocket?"

Hennie held up a mangled scrap of wet, khaki fabric. "Looks that way."

"Weird," I said. "Jerry wanted my muffin, but it looks like he already had one. I guess he really likes muffins."

"What's not to like?" Nolan asked. "Did you get muffins?"

"There's a sample in the office. Kimmy Cakes Bakery was here."

Nolan's eyes widened slightly, but he shook his head, bringing his attention back to the scene. "I wonder what made Jerry sweat so much."

I searched on my phone, but since the cell signal was so weak and I was too far from the Wi-Fi, it took a long time for anything to come up.

When the results loaded, I told them, "There's a disorder where people sweat a lot."

Hennie put her hand on Jerry's bare arm and nodded. "Could be low blood sugar," she said. "He's cold to the touch, and it's too soon after dying for all that."

"Low blood sugar…" When I scrolled, I found it mentioned in a list of possible reasons for excessive sweating.

"My grandmother had diabetes," Nolan said.

"So did my Charles," Hennie said. "When he died, I found him like that—cold and sweaty."

"That's awful." I hadn't known her husband, but it made me sad to think she'd lost him like that. "The only thing is," I pointed out, "muffins are sweet. If he ate one, wouldn't that *raise* his blood sugar?"

"The wrapper must've been from earlier in the day," Nolan said.

"Could be why he wanted another," Hennie added. "Might've been feeling ill if the blood sugar got too low on him."

"Then that means it definitely wasn't murder." A hint of hope snuck its way into my voice.

"Well…" Hennie narrowed her eyes and scrunched her face in thought. "Let's just make sure of that."

"How?"

She held up a finger. "I'll be right back. Don't let anyone near the body." She set the wrapper on the ground. Bubbles of goat vomit stuck to the folds.

I held up my hands. "Uhh…?"

Hennie took off on her four-wheeler before I could explain to her that when the EMTs or police showed up, I'd have to let them into the wildlife area to do their work.

"What could she be doing?" I asked Nolan.

"Never know with that one."

I faced the front of the campground and watched for the ambulance to arrive.

Hennie returned sooner than I expected, carrying a black box the size of a thick book. "I beat those coppers!" she said. "This'll tell us if it's poison."

Hennie set the box down and opened it, then pulled out several small strips of paper. I slid my eyes to Nolan. He reflected my look of confusion.

Hennie moved closer to where she'd dropped the wrapper and rubbed one of the strips against it.

"Can we do one in the victim's mouth?" Nolan asked.

"What!" I slapped his arm lightly. "That's disgusting."

"What better way to know?"

"Fine idea." Hennie jumped over the fence, and I looked away until she jumped back. "Now we wait." She held the strips of paper between her fingers. "Only takes a few minutes."

I looked at Nolan again. No way this could actually detect something.

Hennie consulted a guide sheet that was in the box. After checking her watch, she held the strip close to her face to inspect it.

"Fooey." She set the strips down. "Looks like we got nothing."

"You're disappointed it's not poison?" I asked.

"That would have made things simple." She packed the items back into the box and shut it. "Now how will we solve this?"

"I guess we'll let the police and doctors find out what made him sick and that'll be the end of it," I said.

"And here they come." Nolan pointed to the front gate, where an ambulance and cop car had just pulled in.

I jogged to the gate with Gar in tow and hit the button that manually raised the gate arm. I pointed to Jerry's body. The ambulance drove over the grass to get closer.

I decided to let Nolan and Curtis handle this one. I returned to the office, and Hennie walked in behind me, then Gar. He went into my office and turned in a few circles under my desk before settling into his bed. Hennie leaned her elbows on the front counter and stared at the test strips in her hand.

"What's going on out there?" Sally asked, her eyes stretched wide as she watched Hennie.

I bit my lip. The way Sally reacted when Jerry had entered the store warned me she wouldn't take this well. I stood close to her and took her hands in mine. "I'm afraid I have some sad news."

Her forehead creased and the curiosity left her expression.

"Jerry Bishop is dead. The cops and EMTs just arrived."

Sally gasped and put a hand to her mouth. "But he was just in here! It can't be! What will happen now? What does this mean?" She stumbled back until she found Curtis's old stool and sat hard. She muttered, "He'll never design another purse. How sad."

"Purse?" Hennie asked.

"Jerry was a famous purse designer," I told her.

She harrumphed. "Who ever heard of such a thing."

Sally looked at her and scoffed. "He only made the best purses in the whole wide world!"

Hennie held her hands up in surrender. "I don't doubt it. Just didn't reckon it was something people get famous for."

Sally wiped a tear and crossed her arms, the anger gone and the sadness slumping her frame. "Well, it is, and he was the best. To think, all that talent, gone from this earth forever. His family must be heartbroken." She wiped another tear. "I wanted one of his designs so badly. Now I might never get one." She broke into sobs, and I put an arm around her shoulders.

"I don't know if this makes it any better," I said, "but it looks like he was ill and died. I don't think he suffered, and it doesn't look like anyone killed him."

"Killed him?" Sally looked up at me and sniffled. "Who would do such a thing?"

"No one."

Then she said, "I wonder if the press knows yet. It'll be huge news."

A death in the campground would be big enough, but the death of a famous person was sure to have all of Outer Branson talking. "It just happened, so I wouldn't think so."

The front door opened and a family of campers walked in.

The son, a lanky preteen, said to his younger sister, "I bet someone died. People have died here, you know."

The sister squealed in fright and smacked him.

"Don't scare your sister," the mom said absently, and then, "Don't hit your brother." She looked at the three of us. "Do you have hot dogs?"

"In the cooler." I pointed.

When she walked away, the dad approached us. He asked in a near whisper, "Everything okay out there?"

"Oh, sure. Someone just got sick, but it's fine." It felt wrong to lie, but I wasn't going to tell him in front of his eager son that a dead body was just feet away.

Before the family left, a couple in their forties walked in and headed straight for the chocolate and marshmallows.

"I know, but there have been two murders here," the woman said quietly. She snapped her head to look at me, then quickly looked away.

"I'm sure it's fine," her husband told her.

Sally rang them up.

I added, "Have a great day!" as they walked out.

I pushed the door open and stood in the doorway to judge the status of the wildlife area. It looked like nothing more had happened than the EMTs and cops had gotten out of their cars, left their conspicuous flashing lights on, and started up a conversation amongst themselves. Nolan and Curtis were off to the side, talking with them.

As I stood there, a car pulled in, opened the gate with their key card, and drove slowly by. The whole carful of people craned their necks to see what was happening.

"This is drawing too much attention," I said to Hennie.

"You want me to cause a diversion? I could go shoot off a few rounds in the woods." She patted her gun holster.

I immediately thought of Nolan and what unexpected gun shots might do to him. "No! No shooting in the campground."

"I could let the animals out of the pen. That would be sure to get folks' attention. Maybe they'd think it was the reason for the cops."

"Or it'll look like the campground is completely under-managed and out of control."

I shut the door and glanced at the candy shelves. I'd been craving sugar all day, and the new stress made it even worse. The sample muffin would be a perfect snack. Remembering the taste made my stomach growl.

I searched where I had stood at the front counter when Kimberly brought the samples in, but couldn't find my muffin. I expanded my search, even checking in my office. "What the heck?" I went back out to the register and looked again.

The muffin was gone.

CHAPTER 5

"What's got you stumped?" Hennie asked as I kept up my search around the front register.

"I can't find my muffin. Sally, have you seen it?"

She shook her head.

"Has Ricky been in here?" I asked. The baby raccoon had been my pet for a short time and in that time, managed to destroy both the store and my cabin. He was a known mischief maker around the campground.

Sally shook her head again.

"We just keep getting more mysteries," Hennie said.

"It was right here," I said. "Look, there's even crumbs."

Hennie leaned closer to inspect them and sniffed. "Smells like blueberry."

"It was."

"You can have mine," Sally offered.

She handed the muffin to me, but something didn't sit right in my stomach. I looked at the muffin and its wrapper. The same waxy sort of paper as the one in Jerry's pocket.

"Hennie, did you take photos of the wrapper from the goat?"

"Tons." She handed me her phone.

I swiped through the images, pausing on one that gave me the clearest shot of the side of the wrapper. I zoomed in and squinted at the picture.

"Look at this." I pointed to a faint collection of lines on the wrapper. "Does this look like it could have been fireworks?"

The same set of exploded lines covered the wrapper of the muffin Sally had given me.

Hennie and Sally both inspected the photo and the wrapper.

"I think so," Sally said.

"Oh, yeah," Hennie said. "It's a match! What does that mean?"

"That jerk stole my muffin." As soon as the words were out, I felt guilty for insulting the dead. I added, "He must've been really hungry. And I guess the goat's saliva washed out the ink of the design."

"That's perfect!" Hennie clapped and slid her black box closer. "We can test this muffin for poison and see if anything comes up. It'll be more accurate since we have the whole muffin."

"Poison?" Sally squealed. "I was going to give that to my kids!"

"I'm sure it's fine," I told Sally. "This is more of a way to rule it out than anything else."

Hennie opened the box again. This time, she broke off a piece of the muffin and used a few drops of my melted ice water to mix with it, making a sort of crumb mush in the kit's small container. She dipped a paper strip in and then set it on the counter to wait.

"Dag-nab-it," Hennie said after a minute. "Still nothing."

Sally sagged in relief.

"Exactly," I said. "Because it's not a murder!"

I had said it much too loudly, and my words seemed to linger in the air when the office door opened and a camper walked in.

"Could it be food poisoning, though?" Sally asked. "Have you ever had it? One time, my husband took me to this buffet, and even though he warned me not to eat the seafood, I had to have some shrimp. Well, I was sure I was going to die that night. Maybe Jerry actually did."

"It's possible, but I feel fine," I said.

Hennie raised an eyebrow. "I thought you said Jerry took your muffin."

"I took a bite of it first. When Kimberly was here. She made me."

"She *made* you?" Hennie asked.

I thought back through my conversation with Kimberly. She had been rather insistent. At the time, I felt like I'd make her mad if I didn't at least take a bite.

"She was very pushy," I said.

Sally nodded. "She was. I heard it."

Hennie threw her hands in the air. "There's our first suspect!"

I let out a heavy sigh. "The only thing Kimberly is suspect of is making a contaminated muffin."

"One way to know." Hennie picked up the muffin and stuffed half of it into her mouth."

"Henrietta Schrute, are you out of your mind!" I screeched. "If that muffin killed Jerry, what do you think will happen to you?"

She set the rest of the muffin down. Crumbs shot out from her mouth as she said, "I'm only eating half."

Hennie took a large swallow, then added, "I wanna see for myself. That Jerry looked like he had low blood sugar. Kimmy might use some kinda new-fangled sweetener that affects people weird."

"I wonder if it did anything to my blood sugar," I said. "Who do we know with diabetes who might have a tester?"

"Doesn't Enid?" Hennie said.

"I think you're right."

"Then what're we waiting for?"

Hennie walked outside. I snatched a stack of new flyers from my desk and called Gar to follow before going out to join her. Nolan jogged over to us.

"So, they've ruled it a crime scene," he told me.

"No!" My shoulders slumped. "How?"

"They suspect injury or some other foul play."

"Based on what?" I glared at the officers in the distance.

"Well." Nolan scratched his beard and scrunched up his face. "Partly because a murder has happened here every month since you showed up."

"Since *I* showed up?" My mouth popped open. "I didn't have anything to do with the murders! I can't help it!"

He shrugged. "But they can't ignore it."

"Well, great." I dug my keys out of my pocket. "We're running to Rollie's to have Enid test our blood sugar."

"Okay...?"

"Jerry stole my muffin, so we tested the other muffin for poison," I said. "Nothing showed up, but Hennie thinks Kimberly might be using some kind of sweetener that messes with blood sugar."

"Worth checking out," he said. "Keep your phone on you in case they wrap up before you get back."

"If it's a murder scene now, I'm sure they'll take plenty of time." It looked to me like the body hadn't even been moved yet.

Nolan returned to the scene as we walked toward my cabin. My new-to-me, old, blue Dodge Dakota pickup sat in my driveway. I'd been sad to see my Lexus go, but knew it was for the best. My shiny silver car would have only gotten more beat up in the campground if I kept it. And selling it had given me a small chunk of change to save for something worthwhile.

I lowered the tailgate, and Gar hopped into the back of the truck. I climbed in and yanked the door shut as Hennie slid into the passenger seat. I drove the mile down Cedar Hollow Road to Enid's general store, Rollie's.

We parked in front of the store, which was now decorated with red, white, and blue bunting across the front. Sunny Boy, the old golden retriever who lived there, slept on the wooden stairs outside of the log-cabin building. We stopped to give him a quick pat on the head.

Inside, I looked over the many aisles of the store, but didn't see Enid.

"Hello there!"

I turned toward her voice and saw her standing by the counter under the "Bank" sign. She scuttled toward us carrying a zippered bag.

"Just making a deposit." She wrapped me in a hug, then petted Gar. "So good to see you all."

"You too." Today, her long sweater was covered in knitted yellow bees on a bright blue sky. She must be a fast knitter to be able to make so much clothing. "I have flyers for the Fourth of July event. We were also wondering if you might have a diabetes test kit."

"We do! Aisle 12 has lots of medical supplies someone might need while traveling. You'd be surprised what people forget."

I gave her an apologetic smile. "We don't need to buy one. Just borrow one? We only need to test Hennie and me."

"Oh." Enid looked us both up and down. "You feeling under the weather? Because I can tell you, the diabetes is no picnic."

I let out a long breath before I explained. "We've had another death in the campground, and we think a muffin may be partially responsible."

Enid raised an eyebrow. "Well, come on to the back then and use mine." She toddled away, muttering, "Goodness. Another murder. Who'd have thunk it, right here in little Outer Branson."

I left the pile of flyers on the front counter and followed her. In the backroom, amongst the stacks of supply boxes, Enid took her brightly striped purse from a series of hooks on the wall. I felt relieved to see a handmade, traditionally rectangular purse. She set the huge, knitted bag on the table with a thump and yanked the sides open. After digging inside for several seconds, she pulled out a square plastic device.

"Who's first?" She turned to us with a smile, holding up a small lancet.

Hennie bravely stuck her hand forward and gave Enid her finger. Enid pricked her and put the paper strip with Hennie's blood drop into the device. It beeped a moment later.

"Normal range," Enid announced, then came at me.

I stuck out my finger and flinched when the lancet pricked me.

After the second beep, Enid said, "Also good. Wish I had numbers like yours." She whistled and tucked her kit back into her cavernous purse.

"I guess there was no weird sweetener," I said as we walked out from the backroom. "And wouldn't the muffin taste strange if it had been bad or poisoned?"

"Depends on the poison," Hennie said. "Cyanide has a taste. Bitter almonds, according to Agatha Christie."

"I didn't taste anything like that, did you?"

Hennie shook her head. "It was a good muffin. I like that Kimmy Cakes."

"Oh!" Enid clapped several times. "We just started carrying her muffins and cookies." Her face fell and she asked, "Are they the ones making people sick?"

"Doesn't seem like it," I said. "Hennie ate half of one and is fine. I had a bite, but I'm fine, too."

Enid wagged a finger at me. "Well, you let me know if I need to pull them off the shelf. Whatever happened with your turtle, dear?"

"She moved on. Haven't seen her since."

Enid patted my shoulder. "Very good, very good. If she comes back and you want to take mine over to mate her, he's all yours."

I held my hands up. "No, no. I don't want more turtles. One was enough."

Enid tapped the pile of electric-blue flyers. "I'll hang some of these up. I hope lots of people come."

"Me too. Thanks." My phone buzzed in my pocket, and when I checked it, I saw a text from Nolan.

It said, "The police want the camera footage. Not sure how to do that."

"We gotta go," I said. "I forgot all about the cameras."

Hennie, Gar, and I hurried out of Rollie's and down the road back to the campground. I parked by the office and went inside to find Nolan in my office, looking at the monitor screen.

"You need the laptop to download it," I said.

He stepped out of the way, and I sat at my table desk to open my computer. I found the correct camera and downloaded the afternoon's footage. My cup of ice sat nearby. I chomped a piece as I watched the download progress bar crawl to a finish, then played the video. Nolan and Hennie watched over my shoulder.

On the screen, Jerry stood at the fence, handing food pellets to the goats. He tried to give some to each, but one goat—the one who had later eaten his shorts—kept nudging the others out of the way. Jerry appeared to get agitated—swinging his arms wildly to shoo the goat away—before stepping up onto the lower rung of the fence to throw the remaining handful of feed across the pen. He stood there a moment, gripping the top rail. Then he put one hand to his head and toppled forward, over the fence. He didn't move after that.

I turned to look at Nolan and Hennie. "It's obviously not murder."

"Unless he was poisoned," Nolan said.

"That's just what would've happened if he was," Hennie agreed.

* * *

Later that evening, after we'd finished a dinner of baked chicken and rice, Nolan and I sat on my back deck, drinking beers. The sky was heavy with clouds, making the lights I'd strung along the deck's railing feel as if the stars had fallen down around us. The cool day led into a sticky night. Bugs bit my arms despite the citronella candle on the table.

"Gonna storm tonight." Nolan leaned back in his chair and gazed at the suffocated moon.

"I thought so, too, since it was so cool today." I reached down to pet Gar, who lay on the porch between us. The orange kitten, Blaze, was curled up against Gar's stomach, purring in his sleep. The two other kittens, Ash and Coal, cuddled up together in the corner against the cabin.

"I don't see how the police named it a crime scene," I said, thinking again of the video. "It clearly showed no one there."

"Had to do with the position of the body and how sudden and unexplained the death was."

"Who in the world would have murdered him, though? Sally made it seem like everyone adored him and his purses."

"Maybe someone was jealous or wanted to eliminate the competition," Nolan said.

"Are there a lot of purse designers in Outer Branson?"

Nolan raised both eyebrows high. "You're asking *me*?"

"Have you ever seen me with a designer purse?" I said. "I don't know anything about this stuff, either. My sister got me an expensive handbag for Christmas years ago. My terrier chewed it the first month, and I went back to the cheap knock-off purse that he ignored."

"Still more experience than I have."

I sighed. "If Jerry was poisoned, the killer would have had recent access to him, right? It's not like someone could have poisoned him days ago, could they?"

"Not based on the suddenness of it."

"We know he ate that muffin and that he stole it from me soon before his death." I tapped my foot as I thought. "I mean, the baker seems the most obvious, except that Hennie also ate a muffin and is fine."

Nolan nodded. "And she'd need motive. Unless it was an accident. Some sort of deadly food poisoning that only affected the one muffin."

"Maybe. According to the reservation book, Jerry was camping with a woman. His wife, I assume—Mandy Bishop. She would have been with him before he came to the wildlife area, so she must be a person of interest."

"Then we'd have to include you." Nolan jerked an eyebrow at me. "You supplied the muffin to him, however unwittingly."

I coughed and sat up. "Me?!"

He shifted his gaze back to the thick clouds overhead and smacked his arm to kill a bug. "Sucks to be a murder suspect, huh?"

"They can't possibly think I'm a suspect!"

"I don't think the police will agree with you."

"I guess I could be a person of interest, but certainly not a *suspect*. I have no motive!"

"Oh, I don't know." He rocked back in his chair. "I hear Jerry was a pretty annoying customer, and I know you've been stressed lately. Maybe you snapped."

"Nolan, this isn't funny."

"Just thinking like a cop. You need to be ready to answer these questions."

"All I have to do is tell the truth. I didn't kill him."

"Well, there you go." Nolan took a long sip of his beer and set the can down. "Who was in the store around the same time as Jerry?"

"Just Linda. Crazy loon. The way she threatened me, I wouldn't put murder past her."

"Did she know Jerry?" he asked.

"She had one of his purses, but I don't think she knew him personally."

"Then she's probably not involved."

"Jerry deserves justice if he was killed, and we have to figure out who it could be before the cops start suspecting me. And before it can ruin the Fourth of July event."

"Then I guess you better get your cup of ice and notebook and get those sleuthing skills back out. Looks like you have another murder to solve."

CHAPTER 6

My phone rang much too early in the morning. I reached through my sleep haze to grab it from my nightstand. I blinked at the screen several times before I registered "Forwarded Call" as being important. Gar sat up from his bed on the floor and watched me.

"Cedar Fish Campground, how can I help you?" I sat up and yawned.

A woman told me, "I'm at the front gate. My card worked to open the gate, but there's a... turtle."

I rubbed my face and tried to understand. "I'm sorry, a what?"

"There's a very large turtle blocking the road."

Her words sunk in. I threw the covers off and stood. Gar stood, too, and licked his chops in anticipation. "I'll be right there."

I put my phone down, muttering to myself, "Stupid turtle. Can't believe she's back. What in the world are we going to do with this thing?"

I pulled on jeans, then texted Nolan. "Turtle's back. Just got a call that she's blocking the entrance."

The time on my phone said 5:42. He would be up, but he might still be running or working out.

I picked up my grey hoodie from the floor and shoved my head through the hole. The sliver of sky I could see through my curtains looked to be on the cusp of dawn. Turtle got lucky. If the camper had pulled in when it was earlier and darker, the turtle might have gotten squished.

"Running over," Nolan texted back as I wrapped an elastic tie around my long, brown hair.

"Meet you there."

Gar followed me down the stairs and out the door. When I stepped outside, I knew Nolan had been right. The ground was squishy and sparkling with thick dew. Puddles sat in several places on the paths, and the air smelled clean and fresh. Maybe the rain had brought the turtle out.

My feet hit the paved main road just seconds before Nolan's did. Gar bounced to him and licked the sweat from his hand.

"What are we going to do with this thing?" I asked.

Nolan shook his head, sweat dripping down his temples. His smooth, red tank boasted a large damp spot that stuck to his chest, and the shorts he wore clung just enough to highlight his butt. His bare calves appeared chiseled out of stone.

"Is this what you always run in?" I asked.

He gave a half smile. "You like it?"

I liked the way I could see every muscle of his arms bulging from his recent exercise. I shrugged it off. "Looks comfortable."

He laughed. "It is."

He walked toward the front of the campground, and I trailed a few steps behind as Gar yipped and dashed back and forth across the road. Maybe I could start running, too. It'd be good exercise and didn't involve equipment or going anywhere.

I caught up to Nolan and squinted to see the car in the distance. "Have you ever had turtle soup?" I asked.

"You know they're endangered, right?"

I lifted a shoulder. "If it happens to die, why shouldn't I make some good of it?"

"How is it going to die?"

I huffed. "Haven't you noticed? Deaths tend to happen here."

We reached the woman at the front gate who stood in front of her car. "I tried honking at it, but it didn't budge. I didn't want to get too close."

The turtle opened its mouth to reveal its hook-like beak and then snapped it shut again.

"No, don't go near it." Nolan made a quick assessment of the situation. "Just go ahead and drive around. But go slow. The ground is soft from the rain."

The woman opened her driver-side door, and the light made her parking tag visible. Site 74. Jerry's campsite. I looked more closely as the woman got into her car. Her eyes were red and swollen. She looked exhausted. On the seat beside her sat a bright-purple triangular purse, edged in gemstones.

She drove slowly where Nolan indicated and, though her car left ruts in the mud beside the road, she made it around without incident and waved as she continued down Catfish Lane.

"And now the turtle is causing damage to the property. Great." I put my hands on my hips and glared at the shelled intruder.

"I'm surprised you don't want to make it a pet like you do with every other creature that shows up here." Nolan picked up the free-standing Stop sign and moved it into place in front of the turtle.

"Look at her. She's terrifying. And she doesn't move. Who wants a pet that just sits there looking creepy?"

To prove my point, Gar ran to the turtle, sniffed it, and jumped away before running off to find something else to chase.

"I guess it's time to call the Department of Conservation," Nolan said.

I rolled my eyes. "Like we don't have enough to deal with without the MDC poking around. Do you know who that was?" I jerked my thumb in the direction the car had gone.

"A camper?"

"That was Mandy Bishop. Jerry's wife."

Nolan raised his eyebrows. "She might be here to pack their things up. On my final drive through after I left your place last night, their tent was still there. I can't see her wanting to stay after Jerry died."

"No. And they only had tonight left, anyway." That gave me an idea. "If she's packing up all alone, she could probably use some help. And maybe we could talk to her at the same time..."

Nolan raised an eyebrow. "You want to interview a grieving widow less than 24 hours after her husband's death?"

"I'm not going to interrogate her. Just have a nice little chat. She might appreciate someone caring. And anyway, if she's leaving, we won't have any other chance!"

He shook his head and sighed. "Let's go."

I tapped my thigh to call Gar to me, and we headed down the short loop of Bass Road to Mandy and Jerry's site.

When we approached, Mandy was carrying a suitcase to her car.

I lifted a hand and said, "Hi there. Mandy Bishop?"

She looked surprised, then covered her face and let out a sob as she nodded.

I gulped and glanced sideways at Nolan. We had come mostly to do good, I reminded myself.

I gave a sympathetic smile. "I realized who you were when you drove past. I'm the owner of the campground, Thea. We thought you could use some help packing up."

She wiped her eyes and looked sadly at the campsite. "Jerry did the tent. I don't really know how it goes."

"I'll get it." Nolan got to work pulling stakes out of the ground.

"I'm so sorry for your loss." I put my hand on Mandy's arm for a moment. "If there's anything I can do for you, let me know."

She sniffed and nodded. "I appreciate this. There's so much to deal with."

"I'm sure. My grandmother died a few months ago. The funeral alone took my mother days of planning."

"His family is doing the funeral and packing up his things. I'm not involved in the business or his personal finances. But I've had to make calls and talk to the police and the press."

I pulled my eyebrows together. "Oh, I'm sorry. I thought you were his wife."

She let out a sad chuckle. "We're not married. Jerry used his last name for me sometimes to be cute. It's actually Mandy Rodgers. I'm just his girlfriend."

Interesting. "I see. What a difficult time for everyone."

Nolan had taken the poles out of the tent and was packing everything into the storage sack. Gar hopped back and forth, following Nolan's path from to tent to sack. I should have reminded him beforehand to take his time.

"And it was so sudden," I continued. "Did Jerry have any sort of medical condition or illness that might have caused this? The police haven't told me anything about what happened." It was only partially a lie.

"No. He was a healthy guy. Always checking labels for toxins and things like that. The doctor at the hospital said something about low blood sugar, but I'm not sure what that means."

"Usually, that affects people with diabetes. He didn't have blood-sugar issues?"

"Not that I know of. But I guess his wife might know better than me."

I nearly choked. "Oh, he's married?"

"Yes." She stuck out her lower lip in a pout. "I wouldn't be surprised if *she* did this."

"What makes you say that?" My mind raced with this new information. Girlfriend plus wife and a dead famous man in the middle. It had to mean something.

"She knew he was going to leave her for me. When he told her, she had a fit. They had a huge fight. We came here so he could get away from her for a few days."

My eyes widened. A domestic dispute followed by the husband's death while he's off camping with his girlfriend? My mind screamed, "Motive!" I tried to stay calm and respectful. "When did they fight?"

"They were always fighting, but the big one was a few days ago."

They'd been in the campground several nights now. The fight must've been major.

"I was at the campsite when Jerry died," Mandy said. "I wish I had been with him. Maybe I could have done something."

Fresh tears ran down her cheeks. Nolan stood with the packed tent over his shoulder and tilted his head in a look that said it was time to wrap up. He placed the large sack in the truck and put the cooler in next.

Mandy wiped her eyes. "Thanks. That thing is so heavy."

"No problem." Nolan nodded to her and held a hand up. "If you need anything else, let me know."

She nodded and sniffled.

"So sorry again for your loss." I gave her a sympathetic smile and turned to join Nolan and Gar, who had walked a few feet away.

I waited until we were out of earshot and then whispered to Nolan, "You're never going to believe this! Mandy is his *girlfriend*. Jerry and his wife got in a huge fight days ago when he told her he was leaving her for Mandy. They came here to get away."

"Killer motive."

I rolled my eyes. "Funny. But seriously! We have to find his wife and see what the deal is."

Gar barked several times before taking off at a full run.

"Uh oh. Wonder what he saw." I jogged after him.

"Those cats again." Nolan pointed to a bush where the black and white kitten, Coal, crouched underneath, waiting to pounce as Gar dashed toward him.

Gar chased Coal, and I knew the other two kittens had to be nearby. They were never far from each other.

The turtle hadn't budged from her spot. Now that the sun broke over the horizon, I could see that the muddy ruts beside the road looked worse than I thought.

I paused to inspect the situation. "Can we—?"

"I was just thinking about that," Nolan said. "I think we have a few boards I can put down."

"Thanks."

I continued on to the office while Nolan turned toward the storage shed, Gar at his heels. As I neared the building, I saw movement by the horseshoe pit. Ash and Blaze were at one end, gazing curiously at the ground. I walked closer to see a hole in the sand near one metal stake.

I eyed the kittens. "Did you two dig a hole?"

As I grew closer, I could see what looked like a pile of white ping-pong balls. If we had a ping-pong table, that might explain things. An idea poked at my mind, sparking dread in my chest.

I took out my phone and searched, "alligator snapping turtle eggs." When the results finally loaded, I growled under my breath.

I texted Nolan, "That turtle made a nest and laid eggs in the horseshoe pit. Ash and Blaze are standing guard."

Nolan jogged into sight a short time later, Gar and Coal chasing after him. Nolan stood by my side, shaking his head at the nest.

"Now what?" I asked.

"They'll tell you what to do when you call the MDC."

"Do you think we can just scoop—"

"Nope."

"Well, what if we—?"

"Don't do it. Don't do anything until you call them. You won't believe the fines people face for messing with an animal nest."

I growled again. "It's too early for this."

"Why don't you go get a shower and some coffee while I figure out how to protect the eggs?"

"I wouldn't worry too much about it. If the kittens do something, that's not my fault. I can't be held responsible."

"I'm sure, in all of your lawyering years, you learned something about criminal negligence?"

I narrowed my eyes at him. "I'll be back. With coffee."

My cabin waited for me at the top of a low hill. I followed the path between the playground and pool as the sun lightened the sky. With a long yawn, I went inside and upstairs to shower. I made a cup of coffee and drank it while flipping through yesterday's newspaper. The most exciting thing happening in Outer Branson was the old department store closing.

When my mug ran empty, I headed back to the office. I waved to Curtis, who was walking over from his campsite as I entered the building. In the back office, I started my new coffeemaker. Having only one coffee source at my cabin put too tight a limit on my caffeine consumption, so I'd added another machine a few weeks ago. Life had been much better since.

I opened my laptop and found the number for the Missouri Department of Conservation. Before I called, I did a search on relocating turtle nests. While I found one guide that looked promising, I also found many warnings about turtle mortality rates and needing permits to move nests of protected species.

I sighed and picked up my phone. After explaining my situation and being put on hold for many minutes, I was finally connected to Jeanie Robinson, MDC's wildlife management agent.

"Good morning, Jeanie," I said. "Thea Pagoni, owner of Cedar Fish Campground. We have a turtle situation here."

"Is that so?"

I could picture a smiling face behind her cheerful voice.

She asked, "What sort of situation is that?"

"A female alligator snapping turtle has laid eggs in my horseshoe pit and is sitting on my entry road."

"Oh, isn't that lovely! Would you like to schedule an educator from the MDC to come and give a talk about the turtle?"

"No, I..." They would do that? "Uhh... I want to move it."

"Move it?"

"Yes."

"You can't *move* it." She said the words with heavy shock in her voice.

I went into lawyer mode and stated my case. "Well, the eggs aren't safe where they are. We have tons of wild animals here, including cats, raccoons, and small children. And the turtle on the road is a hazard. She might be crushed by a driver who doesn't see her, or she could cause an accident, which might lead to bodily harm of one or more persons."

The woman huffed twice and then said, "I appreciate your concern. However, I must warn you that if you should disturb the nest, there will be penalties that I don't think you want to face."

I sighed. "Then what should I do? How do I protect the eggs? And I can't have a turtle blocking the entrance to my campground."

"I'm sure the cars can find a way around her. You'd be wise to put up signs to warn motorists and visitors of the turtle and nest. It could be a real attraction, you know. An educator could come and talk to your campers about the turtle. Might bring some good press after..."

I took a stab at where she'd been going with that thought. "After all the bad press we've had?" Great, so she was familiar with Cedar Fish Campground.

"You said it."

"I don't think it would be very good press if an endangered species was crushed by a car or her eggs were eaten by a raccoon." My mind went to Ricky and my eye twitched. I tossed a piece of ice into my mouth and bit hard.

"Again, I appreciate your concern, but neither the turtle nor the nest can be moved. It's too risky."

"Fine." I'd have to get signs and come up with another solution. Maybe she did have a good idea, though... "We're having a Fourth of July event here. What would it take to get someone to come out on the holiday?"

"We don't generally work on holidays, but if you made it worth someone's while..."

I hadn't been prepared for bribery negotiations. "How much are we talking?"

"I'd expect meals for the agent, and you could sweeten the deal with a small stipend."

"We can do that. Multiple talks and time for questions in between?"

"Of course."

"Then it sounds like a deal." We exchanged a few details, and I printed out the email confirmation I received a few moments after we'd hung up. The Fourth event was getting more interesting by the day. I added a note to my files on the event and turned back to the internet to search for custom signs.

After an hour's worth of work, I had a sign on the way that proclaimed, "Turtle Crossing." An illustrated turtle, much cuter than the actual turtle on the road, sat between the words. A second sign said, "Caution: Do Not Disturb Turtle Nest" in bold, red letters.

I closed my computer and left my office. Sally stood behind the front counter, talking with Curtis.

I ignored them momentarily as I pulled open the filing cabinet drawer and flipped through the check-in forms to find Jerry's. He had listed a local address. Most likely, the place he lived with his wife. I folded the form and stuck it in my pocket.

"You might want to come outside," I told Sally and Curtis. "See the turtle nest we now have."

Sally's eyes widened. "She laid eggs?"

I nodded.

Curtis scratched his head. "Isn't that something."

"Someone from the MDC will give talks about it on the fourth. In the meantime, signs are ordered, but until they arrive, we need to make sure no one disturbs the nest or runs over the turtle. Apparently, fines are involved if you do."

Sally's eyes grew even wider. "We need a fence."

"Good idea." I grabbed the walkie talkie as I headed outside with Curtis and Sally.

I took two steps onto the porch and stopped. The wildlife area across the entry road was visible from where I stood. The chickens roamed around their pen, clucking; the deer stood off to one side, drinking from their trough; and the goats were at the fence as usual, trying to get food and attention from the small crowd gathered beside the pen. Flowers and candles covered the ground near the spot where Jerry had died. Several photos of him and a few purses hung on the wooden fence rail. Eight ladies stood in a group, sniffling and consoling one another with hugs.

I raised an eyebrow at Sally. "Do you know anything about this?"

She nodded solemnly. "It's a vigil for Jerry. His death was announced on the news this morning, and it wasn't ten minutes before people in his fan forum started making plans to come. I'd expect a lot more to show up."

I turned back to see a ninth woman join the crowd. With a sigh, I held the button on my walkie to call Nolan. "We have some kind of memorial for Jerry forming at the front. And we need to look at this nest."

"Already there," he responded.

I walked over to the horseshoe pit and saw him at the nest, inspecting it with Hennie and Gar at his side. Gar bounded over to greet us.

"What's this about a memorial?" Nolan asked.

"Jerry's fan club," I said as I petted Gar.

Nolan nodded once and glanced at the wildlife area.

"Jerry musta really been famous." Hennie shook her head at the eggs in the hole. "Got a good-sized nest here. We'll have lots of baby turtles running around in three to four months."

"Three to four *months*?" I almost choked. "They take that long? That's the rest of the summer!"

Hennie nodded. "They should hatch in October sometime."

I rubbed the bridge of my nose. "Can we build another horseshoe pit? Maybe where the old cornhole court was?"

"I think we can arrange that," Nolan said. "I was thinking of putting a few stakes in the ground around the nest and running some chicken wire. Hennie said turtles don't come back to the nest after laying the eggs."

Hennie nodded once in confirmation.

"While you do that, I'm going to talk to Enid."

"And I'm coming along," Hennie said.

Nolan held up a finger in warning. "Don't get yourself into trouble."

"Who me?" I smiled and gave him a quick kiss on the cheek before walking with Hennie to my cabin.

We hopped into my truck and took off to Rollie's.

When we pulled into the parking lot, I confessed, "This is only our first stop. I have what I think is Jerry's home address, where he lived with his wife. But I want to find out if Enid knows them, since they're local."

Hennie rubbed her hands together. "This one sounds like a regular crime of passion!"

"I'm starting to think so."

We stopped to pet Sunny Boy on the porch. Inside, when I saw Speedy—the resident turtle—shuffling down the aisle in his diaper, my hands tightened into fists.

"Hi there, you two!"

I spun until I saw Enid at the front of the store, a bottle of glass cleaner in one hand and a wad of newspaper in the other. She wore a long, red sweater knitted with exploding fireworks across her chest.

"I like the festive sweater," I said as I gave her a quick hug.

"This old thing. Did you bring me some gossip?" Enid asked.

"It might be old news to you," I said. "Jerry Bishop was married. And was at the campground with another woman."

Enid pressed her lips into a line and narrowed her eyes. "Yup. Jerry was a known cheater."

Hennie shook her head. "What a high-quality man."

"Well, and he flaunts it all over town. I hear he takes that Mandy everywhere." Enid put her hand on her hip.

"The thing is, you can't hardly blame him with that wife he's got. Whooee, what a piece she is. Loud. Obnoxious. Demanding. And with all his fame and fortune, it's no wonder he strayed with so many women throwing themselves at him." Enid shook her head and then sprayed the window.

"They throw themselves at him? Because of the purses?" It certainly couldn't have been because of his appearance or personality. He was an average-looking guy, and from what I saw, he didn't even have enough game to charm the goats.

"You don't know about Bishop Purses?" Enid asked. "I don't care for the shape myself, but women go nuts over them. He named each design after whoever inspired the bag. It's quite an honor."

I shook my head. "Nolan thinks the cheating is the perfect murder motive."

"Of course he does, honey. He's a smart man, and anyone can see what happens when these things go on. I wouldn't be surprised one bit if Barbara did it."

"Barbara is his wife?" I confirmed.

Enid nodded as she rubbed circles on the window.

I pulled the check-in form from my pocket and unfolded it. "Does Chestnut Lane sound right for where Barbara lives now?"

"Are you going to talk to her?" Excitement lit Enid's eyes.

"Don't see how we can't," I said.

Hennie added, "I want to see if she's real sad or not. Guilt acts different than grief."

"Keep me in the loop, now," Enid said. "It's all anyone is talking about."

I sighed. "Yeah. I hope it doesn't ruin our Fourth."

"Don't you worry." Enid waved me off. "Anytime someone brings up the death, I'm sure to tell them about the event. Of course, when I point out that they can see where Jerry died, they all become quite interested."

That was one way to get business. "We also now have a turtle nest."

"Oh, boy." Enid glanced over at Speedy, his tail sticking out of his diaper as he scraped away from us. "Just keep them out of your store or you'll never get rid of them."

"I'm trying."

We hugged Enid goodbye and left, taking off toward Chestnut Lane and Jerry's wife.

CHAPTER 7

We pulled up to a large house, well decorated for the coming holiday. Multiple wind chimes in patriotic colors and patterns danced in the hot breeze, creating a chaos of musical clangs. Every bush that lined the walkway was draped in red, white, and blue fabric. We stood on the porch between two plastic mini trees—their tops blue and their bottoms alternating in red and white layers.

I made my expression stoic and empathetic before knocking. After a few moments, heavy thumping echoed behind the door just before it was yanked open. The woman who stood there was tall, wide, and had a mess of curls for hair. She wore a dress that was both too baggy and too tight in various places.

"Who are you?" She looked us both up and down.

I stuck my hand out. "Thea Pagoni. I own Cedar Fish Campground. We've come to pay our respects."

Barbara crossed her arms over her chest. "Funny how I get respect now. My dead husband never gave me any."

I guess I could understand her bitterness, but her boldness about it surprised me. "I'm sorry to hear that," I said. "And I'm sorry for your loss."

Hennie nodded in agreement and hung her head.

Barbara puffed out her chest. "Not sure it's much of a loss."

I gulped and tried to hide my shock. "Has there been any update? Several campers have asked."

"Update? Jerry's dead. What's there to update?"

I glanced sideways at Hennie. She gave a slight raise of her eyebrows.

"Did they discover what killed him?" I'd almost asked *who* instead of what.

"Police are doing an autopsy. Guess we'll know then."

I didn't have weeks to wait for the results. This needed to get solved before the fourth. Time for my own boldness. "Did he have diabetes? I heard that low blood sugar could have been involved."

"Yeah?" She glared at me. "Who did you hear that from?"

"The EMT at the scene," I lied.

Her glare relaxed. "I don't know why Jerry would have that. But I wasn't there that day. He was off with his *mistress*."

I nodded and gave an apologetic smile. "Right. I've... seen her."

Barbara pursed her lips. "He's a cheat and everyone knows it, but he didn't have diabetes. The only thing wrong with him was his stomach condition. I made sure he went to the doctor twice a year, whether he liked it or not. Kept him alive all those years. That little floozy wouldn't do that for him."

"No, I bet she wouldn't. What was the condition?"

"Hypochlorhydria. Low stomach acid. Probably from years of deceit and guilt." Barbara wagged her finger at me and leaned closer. "I'll tell you what really happened. I bet he picked the wrong hussie. Some husband must've come after him and put an end to him, finally."

I nodded. It sounded just as likely to me as Barbara being the one responsible. "Is... Mandy married?"

"How should I know?" Barbara dropped her arms and stepped back. "I have to go."

Before I could respond, she shut the door.

"Wasn't she nice?" Hennie said.

"I guess murder takes the kindness out of a person."

We got back into my truck and drove off.

"She seemed heartless enough to be guilty," I said. "But her idea about some woman's husband isn't bad, either."

Hennie nodded. "Need to find out if that Mandy is married."

"Maybe Enid knows. Though I think she would've mentioned that before."

"What about that hypo-stomach thing? That important?"

I shrugged. "I can't see how a stomach condition would have affected his blood sugar."

When Hennie and I returned to the campground, she went off to her cabin for a while. I strolled toward the office, glancing at the road to see that the turtle had moved, but was still blocking the entrance. The memorial had grown in size, but only five woman stood near the goat pen. Nothing major had happened in my absence, and Sally seemed calm and pulled together.

In my office, I took out my phone and called Enid.

"Rollie's," she answered.

"It's Thea. Got a quick question for you."

"Ooo, what did you find out?"

"Barbara looks guilty, but she also suggested that one of Jerry's mistresses might have been married with a jealous husband. Do you know if Mandy's married?"

"Hmm..." There was a pause, then she said, "Aisle 2," to someone before returning to me. "I don't know for sure, but I don't believe so."

"If you hear anything, let me know."

"Same to you, dear."

I ended the call. Jerry and his wife were near my age in their late thirties, but Mandy came off younger. There was a fair chance she used social media. I opened my laptop, searched for her, and found a profile with Mandy and Jerry together in the photo. In the About section, there was no mention of a husband or ex-husband. A quick glance through the photos showed how excited she was about the purple, gemstoned "Mandy" purse, but didn't reveal any obvious previous partner.

I walked out front where Sally was busy filing paperwork. Curtis had gone on patrol. Back outside, I didn't see Nolan or Gar, so I walked over to inspect what Nolan had done at the turtle nest.

Four stakes were placed around the nest, holding the chicken wire that formed a waist-high barrier. I hoped it would work to keep out curious kittens and raccoons.

I hadn't seen Ricky lately, but he often left little reminders of his presence in piles on the roads. At least it meant we had no issues with food being left behind in campsites. Ricky cleaned it all up, and anything left, the kittens fought over.

I started on an early evening walk through the campground, taking in the sight of many tents and campers and chatting with folks, as I liked to do. That part of my job, more than any other, reminded me of my grandparents. Cedar Fish was their home and their dream, so the campers were family to them, and Grandma and Grandad did their best to make everyone feel like it.

Thinking of them stirred up feelings of loneliness. I missed them and I missed having Gar by my side. He'd been spending a lot of time with Nolan. I walked on, figuring I'd likely come across them both at some point.

I started with the smaller loop of campsites, Bass Road. As I waved and said hello to my campers, I calculated that about a quarter of the sites were full. It was an improvement over where our reservations had been two months ago, but it wasn't enough to make the campground profitable.

A twinge of stress squeezed my heart. I tapped an ice cube into my mouth and chomped it into several pieces. I needed to get new software into place so I could start tracking numbers better. Doing it by hand was time consuming, and I hadn't been able to keep up with everything that the proper software would automatically do. These murders took up too much time.

Maybe I could hire an office manager at some point. I shook my head. We needed a pool person and a second maintenance person before I could afford that. And maybe someone to clean. Nolan was currently covering the bathrooms, showers, and laundry house. I had no one else who could do it and convinced him it counted as maintenance. On occasion, I took over the task for him. But I knew he hated cleaning and didn't do a great job of it. On purpose, I suspected.

A cleaning person was more affordable, since it wasn't a full-time position. It'd be good to have that in place before the Fourth of July. I took out my phone and added "research and advertise cleaning person" to my task list.

I continued my walk on to the camper loop. All was quiet at Curtis's site, but when I neared Nolan's, I heard laughter and loud conversation. Sounded like several men on the back porch. Nolan had mentioned telling some friends about the event. If they had come, I didn't want to disturb them.

I kept walking, but Gar must've sniffed me. He barked and dashed around the corner of the camper, headed for me.

I stopped to pet him and hugged him close. "Haven't seen you all day," I said in my puppy-talk voice. He wiggled in my arms and licked my face.

When I stood back up, Nolan had come around the side of the camper and watched me with a smile on his face. "Perfect timing. I want you to meet some people."

I followed him behind the camper, suddenly nervous at the idea of meeting Nolan's friends. We hadn't met anyone in each other's outside lives.

Two muscular men sat in the chairs on Nolan's porch. They screamed former military in their tank tops and buzzed hair. Their physical builds proved their strength and fitness.

They stood and shook my hand as Nolan gave introductions. "This is Jake and Andre. I served with Jake on my last deployment, and Andre was in the SLPD with me."

"We've heard a lot about you," Andre said.

Jake laughed. "A lot."

I glanced at Nolan, and his cheeks had pinkened. Mine felt warm as well.

Nolan stepped close and put his arm around my shoulders. "Can you blame me?"

I rolled my eyes but smiled. "Good to meet you. Are you staying for the Fourth?"

"Plan to," Jake said.

"I'm looking forward to it," Andre said. "I needed some time away from that city."

Jake looked up at the trees. "It's nice out here. Quiet."

"That's why I'm here," Nolan said. "I can actually relax and enjoy life."

"Me too," I added. "It feels like a different world than St. Louis. That's exactly why I came."

Andre and Jake nodded and tapped their sodas together.

"Well, I'll leave you guys to it," I said. Then, more quietly to Nolan, "I talked to Barbara. Definitely a suspect. I'll tell you about it later."

"Not surprised. Spouses often are." He kissed my forehead and hugged me.

"I'm taking my dog. We're going to walk Walleye Circle."

Andre got to his feet and tossed his can in the trash. "I have a new tent, so I better get started on it."

"Let's do yours, then mine," Jake said.

"Deal." Andre bumped his fist against Jake's.

"Faster with three," Nolan added and joined in the fist bumping.

I smiled before walking off with Gar at my side.

It was good to see Nolan with his friends. He didn't have any guys to really hang with at the campground. I had Hennie and Sally, though Sally always hurried home to her twins and husband after her shift. I wondered if Nolan and Curtis ever chatted or shared a beer.

Gar and I walked around the biggest loop of tent sites, taking time to say hello to everyone we saw. As we finished the loop and walked back down the main road, Andre walked out of the bathrooms. I waved to him and caught up as he joined the path.

"Hey there," I said.

"Hi again."

"Can I ask you something? You were a cop with Nolan, right?" I confirmed.

"I was. Six years."

I nodded and tried to think of a subtle way to ask what I wanted to know. "Nolan doesn't really talk about his cop days much. Or anything from the Marines, either."

"It's easier not to think about some things."

"Right. I know something about that. Did he... enjoy being a cop?"

Andre nodded thoughtfully. "He was damn good at it. I think he liked it. As much as you can like a job like that."

I looked over at him. "What do you mean?"

"It's not easy being a city cop. We see a lot of bad stuff. Lot of terrible things go down."

"Yeah, I wondered about that." I hesitated, then went for it. "Was it something terrible that got Nolan fired?"

"He wasn't fired for nothing good, that's for sure."

"So, you know about that?"

He pulled his mouth into a half smile. "You should ask Nolan."

"I have."

"Ahh." Andre nodded. "All I can tell you is, Nolan is one decent guy. Maybe the most decent I've ever known. You're lucky to have him. And it seems he's lucky to have you."

"Thanks. I hope you guys have a great visit."

I walked away and felt a little relieved, but still unsettled by this question of why Nolan was fired. If he'd done nothing wrong, which is what it seemed like Andre said, then why didn't he want to tell me about it? I had to assume it was because he'd done something he shouldn't have.

Not knowing bugged me. The question of *why* flashed into my mind at the worst times, bringing with it an unease that kept me from fully trusting Nolan. And that bugged me even more. I needed to be able to trust him fully if our relationship was ever going to go anywhere. Not that we were rushing things, but we had been growing slowly closer and hotter as the weeks passed.

Gar and I neared the mini golf and pavilion, which sat just before the horseshoe pit/turtle nest. As the nest came into sight, the movement around it made my heart jump.

"Oh, no!"

I took off at a run. Gar barked and jumped into action. We both reached the nest at the same time.

I leaned over the chicken wire and pulled Blaze out of the hole. "What are you doing!"

He took off and vanished in seconds. Ash and Coal looked up at me from inside the nest's enclosure. Before I could grab Coal, he jumped over the chicken wire and bolted. Ash cowered. I picked him up and set him hard on the ground.

"Leave those eggs alone!"

Gar barked his own reprimand. Ash followed after his brothers and disappeared from sight.

I leaned over to inspect the eggs. I didn't think any of them were missing or broken, but I wasn't going to stick my hand in there to check.

How would we keep the kittens out? They could jump most fences and climb others. Any sort of solid structure would block the nest off completely. That would ruin the whole attraction benefit and could be bad for the eggs to be in darkness all the time. Or would that be better? I didn't know enough about them, but I already knew more than I cared to.

I tried to think of solutions as I went inside to my office. Gar followed and curled up on his bed under the table.

I decided a text wouldn't disrupt Nolan if he was with his friends. And besides, he was technically on the clock.

I texted, "The kittens got over the fence around the nest. Any ideas?"

"I'll rig something up," he responded.

"Thanks. It was good to meet your friends."

"They won't stop talking about you now." He sent an upside-down smiley emoji.

My face warmed as I set my phone down. Keeping our relationship casual had been my desire more than Nolan's, though he'd agreed. Neither of us needed something complicated, but it was nice to know he talked about me to the people in his life.

It made me realize that I'd barely talked to my mom and sister since moving. I hadn't told them a thing about Nolan. They were good at giving me space, but they got busy, too, and sometimes gave me too much.

I sent them each a text just to say hello. Then I added a second text: "Planning a big Fourth of July event. Would love for you all to come out and see what I've done with the place!"

I watched for the little dots showing that one of them was responding, but after a minute, I moved on. They'd text back when they had the chance.

A few minutes after I laid my phone on my desk, my text alert dinged. It wasn't my mom or sister, though.

Nolan texted, "Come get these cats."

I dashed outside and to the nest. Ash was outside of the chicken wire, but Coal and Blaze were back inside. Nolan tried to grab them, but caught air several times. When Blaze saw me coming, he jumped out of the enclosure.

"Coal!" I didn't have to reach in for him. He jumped out and took off with Ash trailing behind.

Nolan shook his head and picked up a square piece of plywood. "I thought this might rest on top of the stakes, but they'll probably knock it off." He set the wood roof in place. "I'll have to secure it somehow, but I just got a call from Sally that there's a flooding shower on the back loop."

"Fix the shower and I'll put the kittens in my cabin until the nest is secure."

Nolan raised his eyebrows. "You're going to catch them and put them in your house?"

"What else can I do?"

"Okay." He laughed and walked to his black pickup.

Gar hadn't followed me outside in the commotion. He must be worn out. He might be more of a hinderance than a help when it came to the cats anyhow.

I spotted Ash hiding under a bush. I approached with caution and called out to him, then squatted and held out my hand.

After a moment of watching, Ash stepped out and trotted over to rub against my hand.

"Good boy." I picked him up and carried him to my cabin.

Finding Blaze and Coal was harder. Blaze especially was good at hiding and getting into places he shouldn't be. After a few minutes of hunting, I resorted to my grandmother's old trick. I retrieved a can of treats from the supply closet in the office and came back outside. I shook the can as I called their names.

Blaze darted for me. He paused to watch the shaking can, then rubbed against my legs and meowed. Coal came a moment later. I kept the noise going as I walked toward my cabin, stopping now and then to check that they followed.

Once I had all three inside, I gave them each a few treats and locked the door behind me. As I turned away, I thought I heard a crash. Through the window, I saw them wrestling each other in the center of the living room. I couldn't just cat-sit all day, so I had no choice but to trust that everything would be fine. There shouldn't be too much they could get into.

CHAPTER 8

I was in my office, deep into my software research, when I heard a familiar voice at the front counter.

Sally said, "Let me just get her for you."

I groaned and crunched the ice cube in my mouth before walking out front. I considered calling Nolan, but he might be with his friends, and I didn't know for sure if I would need him.

I forced a polite smile at Linda Dorsey. "How can I help you?"

"Hello, Thea."

Her voice dripped with sweetness, putting me immediately on guard. "What can I do for you?"

"You can do a lot for me, actually." She took a piece of paper from a folder on the counter. "I came to discuss this."

I glanced at the contract. "There's nothing to discuss."

"I'm sure there's a way we can make this work." She leaned in to me. "I'm prepared to offer you a substantial savings."

"I appreciate that, but the cost isn't the issue."

"Anything can be done for the right price. How about if I take $500 off?" She paused. "$1,000?"

I held my hands up. "If they were free, I still couldn't do it."

Her smile faded. "Don't be unreasonable now. I'm *sure* we can agree on a price."

I placed my palms flat on the counter. "It's not the price. The only fireworks I can have here are silent ones. If you have those, we can talk."

"Silent fireworks? How could there be such a thing?" Her bright-pink nails waved at me. "Fireworks are *made* of explosions."

"I know. And that's why I can't have them. You're finally understanding."

Linda's expression fell into a cold glare. "You think you're so smart. You have no idea, little girl."

I crossed my arms and stood back. "You know, Linda. I've never had to kick anyone out of my campground before. But as they say, there's a first time for everything. Please leave. You and your husband are no longer welcome at Cedar Fish Campground. Do I need to call security?"

Linda snatched up the folder and her triangular purse. A clear cellophane Mint-O wrapper flew out of the yellow, fringed bag. She pointed her dagger-length nail at me. "Just you wait. You'll get what's coming to you."

My eyes narrowed. "I'd watch who you threaten. We had a murder here a few days ago. And it happens that you were in the store right before the victim was. Some might think that's not a coincidence. You could even be a suspect."

Linda's jaw dropped. "A suspect! That's ridiculous! I didn't know the guy who died! I had to read about it in the paper. This is a setup, isn't it? What are you trying to pull? It doesn't matter anyhow. He wasn't even murdered. He just took too much insulin. Sad, but it happens all the time."

"The police are investigating like it's a murder, and I think they would be interested to know that you've now threatened me twice."

Linda crossed her arms dramatically, her permed hair bouncing unattractively as she wagged her head back and forth. "At least I'll know who to blame if the cops come knocking."

She tossed her hair then stomped out of the office, letting the door slam behind her.

I closed my eyes and breathed deeply, glad that the store happened to be empty during that little scene. I shook my head and turned toward Sally.

Her eyes were round circles in her pale face. "Are you okay?" she whispered. "That was terrifying."

"Linda is nuts. If she comes back, call Nolan immediately, then me."

Sally nodded. When the office door opened moments later, she jumped. Nolan walked in and Sally let out a shaky breath.

I smiled wryly and said to him, "Wait until you hear this."

"Does it have anything to do with our new tire ruts?"

"What!" I rushed to the door and pushed it open. Linda must've driven on purpose through the grass, leaving deep ruts in the ground between the parking lot and the main road.

I stormed into my office for my cup of ice. Nolan followed me.

"What's going on?" he asked.

"Linda Dorsey. I had to kick her out. She threatened me again. Don't let her on the property if she comes back." I narrowed my eyes. "Maybe I could sue her for the damage... I'm going to take photos."

"I think it's best to let that one go." Nolan put a hand on my shoulder.

"She flipped out when I said she could be a suspect in the murder."

Nolan laughed. "Why did you tell her that? She wouldn't be."

"I know, but she doesn't. She called me 'little girl.'"

Nolan's eyebrows shot up. "Fightin' words."

I shrugged. "She seemed worried about me calling the police, so maybe that'll keep her away."

"Let's hope. Want a bit of good news?"

"Please."

"The turtle is off the road. She's almost at the pond."

"Good." I glanced at my desk, covered in papers. "I need to get back to work. This event won't plan itself."

A voice called from the next room. "Yoooo hoooo!"

I quirked an eyebrow at Nolan. "Is that Enid?"

We went into the main office as Enid hurried in, waving both hands at me. "Oh, Thea, wait until you hear this!"

A customer walked up beside her to pay for his box of matches. Enid said to him, "Nice day, isn't it?" and then smiled politely at me until the man left the store. The instant the door shut, she leaned in and dropped her voice. Nolan, Sally, and I leaned toward her.

"I just came from the hairdresser," Enid gushed. "Well, you know everyone has been talking about this latest murder. Jerry was always a hot topic of gossip anyway with his purses and all those women he runs around with, but this has just sent people through the roof." She lifted her wrinkled hands in the air and shook them. "So. Bertha told Martha that she saw Barbara at the library. They have a fabulous book club, you know. Well, Barbara was there using the internet since she doesn't own a computer." Enid leaned even closer and chided, "Barbara's not too good with technology, I hear."

I held back a chuckle at her critical tone and glanced at Nolan. Enid had once called me to ask if the internet was down because she couldn't connect to her Wi-Fi.

Enid continued, "Well, Martha said that Bertha said that Barbara was searching for ways to kill someone." She stood back and let that sink in.

"At the public library?" I asked.

"They must have some kind of record of that, right?" Nolan asked.

I shrugged. "Maybe. How long ago was it?"

Enid scrunched her face in thought. "A week or two."

"It's worth looking into," I said. "Any word on the angry-husband theory?"

"Plenty. And more theories are spreading. Everyone around town has a favorite suspect."

"Like who?" I asked.

"Jerry had a different woman every month for a while there. Many of them had husbands. Several of the ladies could have done it themselves. He wasn't the most gracious man."

"*That* guy had a different woman every month?" Nolan asked.

"Don't underestimate the value women put on fashion," I said.

Enid nodded. "And he made it so competitive with the naming. I wouldn't put it past some of them to kill over that. They got so jealous of each other. When the 'Mandy' came out, there was a boycott for a while. Until the lottery winners were announced. The winners all had no problem forgetting about the controversy when they got a chance to buy one."

"Man." I rubbed the aching spot in my neck. "I guess he had some kind of talent if women reacted like that and fought over the chance to buy his items."

"I don't get it," Nolan said. "You can get a purse anywhere. What's the big deal?"

"You can only get a Bishop purse through the lottery. People go crazy over exclusivity and name brands." I tapped my finger against my lips. "We need some kind of ploy like that. I wonder if we could make a luxury campsite and hold a lottery to see who can stay there. Glamping is becoming more and more popular, you know."

Nolan stared at me blankly. "Are you being serious?"

I blew out a breath. "I don't know. But something about Jerry has been on the front page of the *Outer Branson Daily News* every day since the murder happened, and the fan club is taking over the wildlife area. We need to put a positive spin on all this press somehow."

"When you catch the killer, you'll be a hero!" Enid raised her hands to my face. "Then people will pour in. Everyone is already planning to come and see the memorial."

"I need people to camp, not just visit. I've caught two killers so far and it hasn't improved business much."

The three of us looked at each other.

Enid's mouth crept into a sheepish smile. "It's not only the purses, I hear."

"What do you mean?" I asked.

"The women might chase after Jerry to get a purse named after them, but that's not the only reason they stick around."

"He was also famous and rich?" I offered.

Enid giggled and covered her mouth. "Yes, but he was apparently also quite *well-endowed*."

"Is that all women want?" Nolan asked. "They overlook a guy's weirdness for purses, money, and a big..." He gestured toward his pants.

I gave him a crooked smile and quirked my eyebrow. "Are you saying you don't have any of the three?"

He slid his lips into a sly smile. "Wouldn't *you* like to know?"

My face warmed, and I felt hyper-aware of Enid's presence.

She patted my hand. "Easy enough to find out, dear."

"Yeah." I stepped back. "I'm going to head to the library before it closes. Bye, Enid. Thanks for the gossip."

Nolan chuckled as I rushed out the office door.

I shook off my embarrassment and pulled out my phone to call Hennie. "Got a hot tip," I told her when she answered. "Feeling like a trip to the library?"

"You know it."

I waited beside my truck for Hennie to pull up on her four-wheeler. When she arrived, she hopped down and came to me.

"What's the word?" She threw a punch toward my face, and I knocked it away with my forearm. "Good." She slid her feet into fighting stance and put her fists up. "Always be ready."

We practiced a few self-defense moves back and forth, then got into the truck. I caught Hennie up on what Enid told us as we drove. When we parked at the library, we entered and found the librarian at the front counter. Luckily, no one else was in the immediate area.

"Ooo!" Hennie whispered to me, "I know her!"

"Then you talk."

"Hi, Phyllis. How's it going?" Hennie leaned on the counter and smiled. Her long, grey braid fell over her shoulder.

"Haven't seen you at the range much," Phyllis said.

"Can't beat shooting in my own backyard. And I got me an apprentice now." Hennie thumped my back.

Phyllis smiled. "Hi there."

I smiled back. "Nice to meet you."

"Thea owns Cedar Fish Campground," Hennie explained. "Have you heard about what happened?"

"Oh." Phyllis's eyes widened. "Two people were killed there this summer."

"Three, actually," I said.

"Oh." Phyllis nodded and her mouth hung open in shock.

"We need to put a stop to all this, you see," Hennie continued. "And you can help us."

Phyllis put her hand to her chest and drew her head back. "Me?"

"We know who did it, but we need proof," Hennie said. "You know that Barbara Bishop who's married to Jerry Bishop?"

"The purse guy?" Her eyes darted to me and back to Hennie.

"Yeah, him," Hennie said. "He's dead. And it looks like Barbara offed him."

Phyllis sucked in a breath. "Can't say I'm too shocked by that."

"No one is. Someone saw Barbara in here on the web, looking up ways to do the deed. We need to print that out for proof."

Phyllis looked around, then turned to her computer and concentrated on typing. "Here's her account. Oh, but this only shows her check-out history."

"Wouldn't you need to get on the computer to see the browsing history?" I suggested. "Like through an administrator account or something?"

"Oh!" Phyllis searched a pile of papers on the corner of her messy desk, then set an index card on the counter in front of us. "Here's how we log in. Do you know how to do all that? I don't, and Leslie isn't here. She knows all that stuff. She's the library director."

"I can try." I picked up the index card and found an empty computer station in a somewhat secluded area. None of the computers offered much in the way of privacy. Not the best place for searching out murder details, but apparently, that's all Barbara had. Hennie and Phyllis watched over my shoulder.

I clicked around until I found a program that made me log in. The info on the index card worked, and I was in an admin account. I looked through some things in the program, but didn't really know what I was looking for, so I opened the browser and checked the history. Nothing there.

"Does the history automatically clear when someone logs out?" I asked.

Phyllis nodded.

"Then I don't think this will help us." I looked up at the ceiling. "Are there cameras?"

Phyllis shook her head.

"Maybe there's something in her check-out history," Hennie suggested.

Phyllis looked around and smiled at the other patrons using the computers. "Oh, but I can't give out that information." Then to Hennie and me, she gestured subtly with her head for us to go back to the front counter.

Once we were away from anyone who could overhear, Phyllis whispered, "I could get into trouble, so I had to pretend." She typed away and then grinned. "Got it."

She pushed up from her chair and made her way to a small printer behind the desk. When the pages shot out, she picked them up and slid them to us. She pointed to one of the books. "Look at this one."

The title was *Identifying Dangerous Plants*. As I looked down the check-out history, many plant-related titles were listed.

"She was a gardener?" I asked.

Phyllis nodded. "It would have been easy for her to grow the right plant to poison Jerry."

"Is the book here?" I asked.

Phyllis tapped a few keys, then stood. "It is!" She scurried off, disappeared into the stacks, and returned a minute later with a large, thin book. She set it on the counter.

I paged through it, looking at the photos. Each page showed one photo of a plant, and its facing page gave information about it, including any effects from consuming it.

"This is perfect. Can we check this out?"

"Do you have a library card?" Phyllis asked.

"I don't."

I looked to Hennie. She shook her head.

"You'd need a library card," Phyllis said.

"How do I get one?" I asked.

"Provide something that proves you live or work in Outer Branson."

I hadn't changed my driver's license yet, but I had the little change-of-address card the DMV sent me. I handed it to her. "Does this work?"

Phyllis looked at it, then handed it back to me. "Afraid not. Do you have a copy of a utility bill?"

"Can I show you a digital one or print it from my email? I pay my bills online."

Phyllis pressed her lips into a line, and her friendliness faded. "Now, I can't be breaking the rules and giving just anyone a library card. That card gives the holder a lot of power."

I blinked at her. "But you know I own the campground, and you know Hennie lives here. You're already..." I looked around to make sure no one would overhear. I leaned in and whispered just to be safe. "You're already breaking the rules by showing us the history."

"Some things I can't make exceptions for, and giving out library cards is one of them." She crossed her arms and hardened her face.

I nudged Hennie's leg with my knee. She finally spoke up. "I know you're doing your job, Phyl, and you're doing a mighty fine job of it. But this here is murder we're talking about. What if you give Thea a card and let her take the book, and she'll be sure to bring back a bill so you can copy it and keep it on file."

"When?" Phyllis demanded.

"I'll bring it tomorrow," I said.

She considered, then narrowed her eyes. "Fine. But you better bring it. I'm going out on a limb here, giving you this card."

She typed a few things into her computer and then slid a form my way. "You'll need to fill this out in its entirety."

I got to work on the extensive form while Hennie flipped through the plant book. "Some good ones in here."

After many minutes and many filled-in boxes, I signed my name at the bottom of the form and handed it back to Phyllis. "I'm surprised they don't ask for your signature in blood."

She took the form with an unamused expression.

I turned my attention to the book while Phyllis entered my information. After a few minutes, she handed me a plastic card.

"Now, don't lose it. If you lose the card, anything checked out with that number is your responsibility, whether in your possession or not. Do you understand?"

"Yes. I'll guard it carefully." I slid the card into my back jeans' pocket.

Phyllis shook her finger at me. "And bring that bill. I won't have my boss checking up on me and catching me doing something unethical."

"Right. I'll make sure of it."

"Tomorrow," she said.

"Tomorrow."

Phyllis scanned the barcode and handed the book to me. I took it and grabbed Hennie's arm. "We better let Phyllis get back to work. Thanks!"

Hennie waved goodbye as we made our way back to my truck.

"I think it was easier to get divorced," I said as I slid in behind the wheel and set the book on the seat between us.

"Stealing library books is a federal offense." Hennie nodded once. "Serious business."

"You sure about that?"

"There was that John Gilkey guy. He went to prison for stealing books."

"I don't know who that is, but I don't plan on stealing any books. I just want to have it with us when we sneak to Barbara's tonight and look through her garden."

"Woo! I like how you think, lady!" Hennie licked her lips. "We got us some real crime now. Trespassing, stealing library books—what's next?"

"I'm not stealing library books!"

She leaned over and eyed me up and down. "That's what they all say."

I put my hand to my forehead and pulled onto the main road. "We'll have to wait until it's dark. And don't tell Nolan."

"Oh, no, we'll keep loverboy out of it."

"He's not my... lover."

"Yet." Hennie wagged her eyebrows at me.

"I don't think that's going to happen anytime soon."

"Aww. Poor guy. Poor *you*."

"Our relationship just isn't like that."

Hennie smirked. "I see the way you ogle him."

"I don't ogle."

She leaned back and crossed her arms. "Oh, you ogle. Practically drool."

"I'm allowed to look."

"But what fun is looking if you ain't touching?"

"Plenty. Now you. Get to work. What do you think our most likely plants are?"

Hennie picked up the book and flipped pages. "Here we go! Lavender is your answer."

"Lavender is dangerous? Since when?"

"It's in here for drug interaction warnings. Here's the good part." She tapped the page. "They call it the 'herb of love' because it's a natural aphrodisiac."

"We are not researching herbs that will affect my love life."

"If you got some now and then, maybe you'd be less stressed and could focus more. Just saying."

"Let's stick to poisons and leave my sex life out of it."

CHAPTER 9

Nolan was hanging out with Jake and Andre that night, which worked just fine for my plans. Hennie and I needed the cover of darkness so that we could sneak around Barbara's house unseen. If Nolan was with his friends, he wouldn't realize I was gone or be thinking about what I was up to. I had dressed all in black and kept Gar quiet with a bowl of food.

I waited in my truck at the campground exit, just as we planned. Jerry's fans had all gone home for the night, so no one would see us leave. Hennie opened the passenger door and slid in. She wore all black, too. The ski mask pulled down over her face gave her the appearance of an owl, her round eyes sparkling with excitement.

"I don't think we'll need all that," I said.

"Never know who has a camera."

She made a fair point, but I didn't own a ski mask. "I'll pull my shirt up over my face when we get there."

"Put these on, too." She handed me the pair of sunglasses sitting in my console.

When we neared Barbara's, we parked several houses away before quietly leaving the truck. There wasn't much to cover us in the way of foliage, and I felt exposed as we walked along the road to the house.

"Let's go through backyards," I said.

Hennie followed me down the nearest yard and then we continued through two more before we reached Barbara's. I lifted my sunglasses to get a better look around.

"Looks like she has a nice garden." I pointed to the area full of staked leafy plants.

We crept closer. Hennie took out her flashlight and shined it over the garden sections.

"Tomatoes, peppers, green beans." Hennie swept her light back and forth. "It's all regular plants."

I looked around the rest of the yard, squinting to see in the darkness. "What about that flower bed?"

On either side of the backdoor, a bed of flowers stretched along the length of the house. We moved closer to inspect them.

"Ah ha!" Hennie whispered and pointed her beam on a plant with tiny, white flowers.

"Queen Anne's lace? Is that poisonous?" I asked.

"Don't know, but this ain't Queen Anne's lace, it's water hemlock. Often confused. Also deadly."

"You sure?"

"It was in the book."

I'd left the book in the truck. Smart. I pulled out my phone and searched for water hemlock. When the photo came up, I agreed with Hennie that we had something.

"Let's take some." I reached for it, then pulled my hand back. "Will it harm us to touch it?"

"Maybe." She slid a black knit glove on her hand before breaking the stem of the flower off near the ground.

I took a photo of the remaining cluster of plants. The flash looked much too bright and startled me. "Shoot. Let's go before someone sees us."

Hennie and I hurried back through several yards to reach the truck. As I drove away, she searched the book.

"Here it is." Hennie held the page up for me to see. "Highly toxic. Can cause serious harm to people and animals."

"I'd say that solves it then."

"But nothing came up when I did that poison test," Hennie pointed out.

"Does it look for things like that? And how accurate is that test anyhow?"

"It's plenty accurate. I watched a YouTuber review it and everything."

"Maybe it's one of those things that can't be easily detected, and that's what makes it so good for poisoning. Plus, it looks like a common flower, so it's easy to hide."

Hennie nodded and set the flower on the dashboard. "Definitely a possible clue. Except we got it by illegal means, so we'll have to do some fancy talking around that."

"Right." I'd have to somehow mention it to the police while making it seem like I'd seen it when we were at Barbara's house before.

"How does water hemlock work?" I asked. "Did Jerry have the signs of being poisoned by it?"

"Doesn't really say in the book." Hennie tapped at her phone a while then said, "Seizures, vomiting, dizziness, and abdominal pain."

"I don't think Jerry had any of that. Except maybe dizziness."

"Maybe Barbara used something else then."

We pulled into the campground, and I swiped my keycard to open the gate. I watched the road for a giant, spiky shell, but saw none.

"I wonder about that baker woman," Hennie said. "She might be in on it with Barbara. They might've baked up a scheme together."

I parked in front of my cabin and shut the engine off. "I don't think Kimberly is connected to Jerry in any way. I do need to talk to her about cupcakes, though. Wouldn't hurt to bring him up and see how she reacts."

"Cupcakes for breakfast then?"

"Sounds perfect to me." We bumped fists and Hennie got out of the truck. She tucked the flower carefully into her shirt pocket before driving off on her four-wheeler, waving.

As I approached my front door, I heard barking and scurrying inside. Not a good sign. I opened the door to chaos.

Gar dashed back and forth in the kitchen, barking at Coal, who stood in the center of the kitchen table, his tail poofed and back arched. My lamp and books had been knocked off my end table, and a framed photo of my grandparents sat on the floor—the glass shattered. Ash lounged on the couch, cleaning himself innocently. Or so I thought, until I spotted the trail of black leading from him to the fireplace. The fire screen had been knocked down and Blaze sat inside, digging in the ashes. Tiny black paw prints formed patterns across my cabin floor.

"Gar!" He came to me, but growled and kept his gaze trained on Coal, who was still on the table.

My grandmother's crystal vase stood dangerously close to the cat's black and white leg.

"Coal. Don't you knock that vase over." I inched closer to the table.

Coal tensed, then plunged into the air, pushing off the table hard enough to make it shake. The vase wobbled. I lurched for it. It tipped over before I could get there, but landed safely on its side.

I snatched up the vase and inspected it. No cracks or chips. "You got lucky." I wagged my finger at Coal, who now sat on top of my sofa, forming a new spot of black smudges from his dirty paws.

I opened the door to let Gar out. He'd been inside long enough and would be in the way while I tried to clean.

"It's much too late for this mess," I told the kittens. "Good thing you're so cute." On cue, Ash twisted on his back and showed me his grey and white belly. His large kitten eyes begged me to pet him. I glared and retrieved cleaning supplies from under the sink.

I started with the fireplace. Once I had the screen back in place and had swept up the pieces of charred wood and ash from the floor, I went for the kittens.

I held a damp rag and approached my most passive victim. I took hold of Ash's legs and wiped his paws. He struggled against me, batting at my hand like it was a game. I came away with a few thin scratches, but at least I had one down.

The other two weren't as easy. Every step I took toward Blaze sent him running farther from me. I almost had Coal several times, but he slipped my grasp at the last minute. I gave up after a while and sat down.

Minutes later, both Blaze and Coal walked over to rub against my legs. I waited until he was thoroughly distracted, then snatched Coal, wiped his paws, and released him. I grabbed Blaze next, and as I set him down, there was a loud clang from the fireplace. I turned to see Coal, who had just knocked over the screen, batting at a piece of char.

Instead of repeating my steps over and over in a fruitless quest to clean my cabin, I dropped my damp rag on the coffee table and went to let Gar in. He chased the cats, and I ignored them all to go up to my bedroom. I stripped down, but didn't bother getting into my pajamas before flopping onto my bed and falling asleep.

CHAPTER 10

When I walked downstairs in the morning, I saw the paw prints and cringed. I'd managed to forget about the mess downstairs while I'd been getting ready.

I texted Nolan, "Is the turtle nest secure? I gotta get these cats out of here."

"Should be."

I opened the door and waited. It only took a minute for all three cats to run out. When their little tails bobbed out of sight, I returned to my task of cleaning. Despite Gar's repeated pouncing on the mop, I'd finished the hardwood floor and spot-cleaned my couches by the time the coffee finished brewing.

After pouring a steaming cup, Gar and I headed down the path from my cabin. He ran ahead of me, out of sight. I heard barking moments later. I jogged to catch up to where he stood, still barking at the turtle beside the fenced-off nest.

I'd been told that alligator snapping turtles didn't return to their eggs after laying them. So, what was she doing back? And was she trying to get to the eggs behind the wire?

I sent another text to Nolan. "The turtle seems to want to get to her eggs."

He responded, "Turtles don't return to their nests."

"Then our turtle is special, because she's right beside it."

Hennie arrived on her four-wheeler as I waited for Nolan. She stopped in front of me and squinted at the nest. "She's back, eh?"

I held my hands up in surrender. "Do we need to take the fence down so she can get to the eggs? I don't know what to do with this thing anymore."

"They don't usually come back after laying." Hennie walked over and put her hands on her knees as she bent down to inspect the turtle.

"I know, but she did. So, what does that mean?"

Nolan walked into view, but was still several feet from us.

Hennie stood up. "Some kind of instinctual thing, I'd say."

I rolled my eyes at Nolan as he came into speaking distance. "Apparently, our turtle has some kind of super mothering instinct and is the only turtle ever to return to her eggs after laying them."

Nolan rubbed his beard as he considered. Then he shrugged. "See what the MDC says, I guess."

I sighed and turned to Hennie. "Ready to go? She should be open by now."

"Where you off to?" Nolan asked.

Hennie rubbed her belly. "Cupcakes for breakfast. Can't wait."

Nolan's eyes widened. "Cupcakes?"

"We're ordering from Kimmy Cakes for the event. And I want to ask her some things, see how she reacts."

"For the event," Nolan repeated. "So, you'll want me there to make sure they're good, right? To make sure I think other vets will like them?"

I put my hands on my hips. "You didn't really think I'd go to a bakery and not bring you something back, did you?"

He grinned and patted his stomach. "You do know the way to a man's heart. Still, I should probably come along and see all the options."

I chuckled. "Alright. Let me just tell Sally."

I entered the office. Sally stared at her phone like it was about to explode in her hand.

"Everything okay?" I asked.

She nodded, but didn't take her eyes away from the screen. Then I remembered what day it was. "The purse lottery is today, right? They're still doing it?"

"Yes." She glanced at me and chewed her lip. "I'll get a text notification when they have the results."

"I hope you get in."

She sucked in a shaky breath. "I don't know. I thought Jerry staying here was a sign that I would be chosen. But if that was a sign, what does it mean that he was killed here?" Her lower lip trembled as she looked to me for an answer.

I shrugged. "I think it's just a coincidence."

The phone dinged, and Sally jumped hard enough to drop it. She scrambled to pick it up and tapped on the screen, then sighed. "Just my babysitter. The boys colored on the wall again."

"Oh, no!"

She covered her mouth and giggled. "What they don't know is, after the second time they drew on the walls, I got whiteboard paint. The marker just wipes off!"

"That's pretty brilliant."

Sally beamed.

I jerked my thumb over my shoulder. "Nolan and I are headed out. Call me if you need anything. And good luck."

"Thanks!" She tapped her phone screen, then resumed staring at it.

I walked back outside, and the three of us climbed into my truck with Nolan stuffed into the backseat. I drove us to Kimberly's bakery. We entered the shop to the smell of sugar and vanilla. Nolan and Hennie went to look in the glass display while I waited at the counter for Kimberly, who was with a customer.

My gaze traveled along the bubblegum-pink-and-white-striped wallpaper to the glittery cake stand in the corner. The tall wedding cake on display was an ombre of pink layers, covered with a generous helping of silver sparkles. The entire shop looked like it had been dipped in cotton candy, then sprinkled with glitter. The scent reminded me of a vanilla lotion I once had. My stomach gurgled, and I glanced over to Nolan and Hennie, who excitedly debated cupcake flavors.

When Kimberly finished with her customer, she beamed at me. "Hi Thea! So good to see you again! Are you here about some cupcakes?"

"I am. I've decided to order a few hundred for my event. Is there still time?"

"Let me double make sure." She picked up an electronic tablet from the counter and tapped at its screen.

She was not only digital, but mobile as well? I really needed to get Cedar Fish a better computer system. How in the world the campground had survived so long without online bookings or digital reservation tracking was beyond me.

Kimberly looked up with a grin. "I can deliver them to you the morning of the fourth. Does that work?"

"That's exactly when I need them."

"Great!" She clasped her hands together and stepped over to the display case. "These are our most popular flavors, but of course, *anything* can be custom made."

"What do you guys think?" I asked Hennie and Nolan.

"We've narrowed it down to six options," Nolan said.

"Six?" I coughed in surprise. "What are they?"

Hennie held a small napkin with handwriting on it. "Lemon Cream Dream, Over the Carrot Top, Mocha Me Crazy, Sparkling Pink Lemonade, Peanut Butter Overload, and Key Lime Sublime."

I blinked at them. "And I was thinking we'd go with vanilla and chocolate."

Hennie and Nolan looked at me, mouths hanging open in bewilderment.

I checked the display case. Kimmy Cakes must have twenty flavor varieties available. All had cutesy names and looked to be decorated in a quite fancy—and likely expensive—way.

"There are bulk discounts, right?" I asked Kimberly.

She nodded enthusiastically.

"You guys think the masses will like those flavors?"

"If we go with all six, we improve our chances of people liking them," Nolan said.

I sighed and told Kimberly, "Then I guess we need samples of those six flavors."

"Sure!" She turned to pick up a pink box and placed the first cupcake inside.

"And you have different festive wrappers, you said?"

Kimberly nodded. "No fireworks. I remember. I have red and white stripes, blue with stars, and I think I have a few left with tiny flags on them. They're on the featured cupcake, the Ultimate Americana."

"Which one is that?" I asked.

"It's in the featured display." Kimberly pointed to another, smaller case a few feet down.

Nolan and Hennie exchanged looks and rushed to the other case. They muttered something amongst themselves as they peered through the glass.

"Wait!" Nolan held up a hand and looked back at us. "Have to try one of these, too."

I walked down to look over their shoulders. Inside the round display, cupcakes towered high, each one wearing the wrappers with tiny flags that Kimberly had mentioned. From the outside, they looked like a basic cupcake with white frosting, red and blue sprinkles, and a glittery star sticking out the top. The real pizazz was hidden.

On the top circle of the display, one of the cupcakes had been cut open to reveal what lay beneath the wrapper. The top layer of cake was vibrant red, then a creamy white middle layer, followed by a bright blue bottom layer. According to the description card, it was flavored strawberry, vanilla, and blueberry. "The flavors of America," apparently.

"They are quite... festive. Do they cost more being the featured cupcake?"

Kimberly smiled. "There is a bit of an up-charge since it's more time-consuming to make the layers."

"Of course." They looked awesome, but I wasn't going to go broke on cupcakes unless it was worth it. "We'll need to sample one of those, too."

Kimberly took one from the display and added it to the box. She set the box on the counter and pointed to a smaller counter across the room. "There are napkins and forks and knives if you want to sit and have a taste."

Nolan grabbed the box, and he and Hennie were at a table before I could finish thanking Kimberly.

I wanted to join them, but since the shop was currently empty, I decided to use that to my advantage and talk to Kimberly more.

"So, has business been okay?" I asked.

"It's been great! I've been taking samples all over town and people love them."

"Good, good. I wasn't sure if the murder affected things."

She pulled her eyebrows together in concern. "Why would it?"

"Well, with one of your muffin wrappers being found on the victim and all. Some people might think the muffin was involved."

She sucked in a breath and stepped back. "Do people think that? I didn't even know. How did he get it? How does the public know?"

"Nothing stays quiet long in this town."

She gulped and her face paled. "Gosh. I don't know what to say. I mean, how could my muffin have anything to do with a murder?"

I lifted a shoulder. "Food poisoning?"

"But, but—" Her head shook side to side the tiniest bit and her gaze drifted to a spot beside me.

"Like you said, it hasn't affected business, so I'm sure it's fine."

She snapped to attention and focused on me. "Thea, you have to do something for me. You're a businesswoman. You understand. If anyone asks, lie. Tell them it was a store-bought muffin and a generic wrapper. I can't have people knowing that I'm connected in any way."

"Would people think you were involved for some reason?"

Kimberly pulled her head back. "I can't think of any reason at all why they would think I wanted Jerry dead. I mean... No reason. At all."

She seemed adamant. A little too adamant.

"You knew him?" I asked.

She shook her head with wide eyes.

"Then I guess there's nothing to worry about."

"Right." She gulped. "Nothing at all to worry about..."

She breathed faster and let her stare roam across the room.

"You gotta taste this one!" Hennie held up a piece of cupcake and waved me over.

I left Kimberly standing at the display case, wiping the same spot on her counter over and over, lost in a daze.

"Something's up," I whispered to Nolan and Hennie as I joined the table.

Nolan pushed a wrapper containing a piece of cupcake at me. "Eat this."

I put the green cupcake in my mouth. The taste of key lime melted over my tongue. With the sweet, creamy icing to balance out the tang, it was the perfect combination.

"Are they all that good?" I asked.

"That's our least favorite," Hennie explained. "Try them in order."

I ate several more pieces of cupcake, leading up to the featured red, white, and blue one. By the end, my stomach hurt and my teeth ached from all the sweetness.

"I like them all." I sat back and rubbed my belly. "I guess we have to go with the patriotic one. Maybe a sampling of the other flavors to supplement?"

"Can't have too many," Nolan said.

I patted his hand. "I know you'll help me with any leftovers. Can we get back to the murder solving now? I talked to Kimberly."

Hennie wiped icing from her mouth and put on her serious face. "How'd it go?"

"She seemed very nervous. I think we should try to see if we can find anything suspicious."

"We're on it," Hennie said.

"I'm going to place our order and keep her distracted. You guys do your thing."

I walked back over to the counter where Kimberly was busy folding pastry boxes.

"We're ready to order."

"Oh, okay." She picked up the tablet and tapped it again, then asked me questions about the order.

When I saw Nolan and Hennie get up, I took a step to my left so that Kimberly's attention was directed away from where they were headed. Nolan opened the cabinet doors under the counter as Hennie went inside the backroom. My heart leapt.

"So, how much room will I need to display these?" I asked to keep Kimberly's attention on me.

"I wouldn't recommend setting all of them out at once. An assortment of each flavor on a decorated table usually works best. You could rent a display tower if you want to stack them."

"That sounds like a good idea. Can you deliver that with the cupcakes?"

"Sure."

Hennie came out of the backroom, but on her way, knocked over a metal bowl. Its loud clang made Kimberly's head whip in that direction.

"Hey, what are you doing!" She rushed over as Hennie hurried away from the door toward Nolan, who pretended to be getting napkins. "Were you in the back? That's not for customers!"

Nolan said, "Just getting napkins."

At the same time, Hennie explained, "Looking for the bathroom."

Kimberly pointed to a door in the corner clearly marked, "Restroom."

"Oh, there it is," Nolan said to Hennie. "Thanks."

Kimberly put her hands on her hips and turned back to me with an accusatory glare. "What is going on here? Why are you asking these questions about the murder and sneaking around? Are you trying to set me up?"

"No, of course not," I said. "We just wanted to order cupcakes and I guess use the bathroom. Sorry for the disturbance."

She narrowed her eyes. "Your order is all set. I think it's time you folks move on with your day."

"Right. I'm sure you have lots to do."

Kimberly held her glare. I'd never seen her look uncheerful. The sight gave me chills.

I gestured to Nolan and Hennie. Nolan snatched up the box with the remaining bits of cupcake, and we left the shop.

We got back in my truck and pulled away before I went over in more detail how Kimberly had reacted.

Nolan swiped the bottom of the box and licked icing off his finger. "We didn't find anything. I think she's clean. Man, these are good."

I flicked my gaze over to him. "If you start licking the box, I'm taking it from you."

"Can't blame a man for enjoying something tasty." He sighed contentedly, set the box down, and patted his belly. "That was a lot of cake. What's for breakfast?"

"Is there any end to your stomach capacity?"

"Haven't found it yet."

Chapter 11

My sugar overload from the cupcakes led to a hard crash late morning. I drank more coffee than most days and tried to stay awake at my desk as I narrowed down my choices for new software. With all that the campground needed to do and track, it had become more of a task than I anticipated. At the same time, I felt excited over all the things the software would help us improve.

I'd been staring at my laptop screen, my eyes growing heavy, when Sally burst through my office door shouting, "I got in! I got in!"

I jerked awake and stood up as she wrapped her arms around me in a tight, excited hug.

"I got in the lottery!" she squealed again.

She let go of me and danced in little circles behind the front counter. Her hands went into the air and wiggled as she twirled and sent the skirt of her sundress billowing out around her. She put both hands to her cheeks and sighed happily. "I just can't believe it! I'm going to have a Bishop purse!" She shook her fists in the air and let out a loud, "Woo!"

"Congrats!" I clapped and chuckled at her enthusiasm. "Do you know which one you'll get?"

"Oh, yes. I've had it picked out for months! Do you want to see a picture?"

I nodded and waited as she tapped her phone. She held the screen so I could see it.

The "Gloria" was a bright-yellow leather purse with small, round magenta flowers scattered across the front. In the spaces between the flowers were little square brads in bright green. I blinked in surprise. Was she serious? Sally was about to spend several thousand dollars on a purse that resembled a slice of pizza?

"Oh, wow." I scrambled to think of something nice to say. "It's... so colorful and cheery."

"I know." Sally clutched the phone to her chest and looked off with a dreamy gaze.

"I can't wait to see it." Maybe it would look better in person.

I left Sally to revel in her good fortune and returned to work for another hour before stopping to eat. After lunch, I took a long walk with Gar. The fresh air and exercise refreshed me. I nodded and waved to campers as I walked along the looping roads.

I still had to figure out a way to tell Nolan that we had more proof of Barbara's guilt, but without confessing to my little trespassing crime. Every time I got myself involved in solving a murder, he issued the same warning—don't do anything illegal. Could I just go back to Barbara's house to talk to her more and pretend that I saw the water hemlock then?

I had no better answer by the end of the day, and I was too tired to think about it anymore. Not long after I closed up the office and store, I crawled into bed. A nice, early night, and I'd be able to come up with something in the morning.

It might've been a good plan. But at 2:13, my phone rang.

I reached for it and took a moment to locate it before bringing the phone to my ear. "Someone better be dead," I told Nolan. The words left my mouth, and I instantly regretted them. "Please tell me no one is dead."

"No one is dead. But someone broke into the office."

"What?" My heart jolted me awake. "Are you down there?" I jumped out of bed and Gar got to his feet, alert and ready. I pulled on my jeans with one hand.

"I'm here with Andre and Jake. The police are on their way."

"I'll be right there."

I hung up and finished dressing. Burglary now? I hoped it would turn out to be another Ricky incident, but with two ex-cops looking over things, that hope was a dying ember.

Gar dashed with me down the path to the office.

All the lights were on, and I found Nolan inside with his friends. I took a moment to observe the store. Nothing looked to be out of place at all.

"The register." Nolan pointed to where it sat on the front counter.

The bottom of the register, where the money till was, had been busted open. The drawer stuck out at an angle and all the bills were gone. The change compartments still contained coins.

Nolan added, "They tried to get into the safe, but couldn't."

"How'd they get in the building?" No windows had been broken and the door hung properly on its hinges.

"There's some damage around the lock. It looks picked."

"Someone lock-picked the deadbolt? Is that possible?"

He gave a sad smile. "It's easier than you think."

Well, great. Now I would never feel 100% safe. "I'll look into more secure locks, I guess. Did you watch the video yet?"

He shook his head. "I waited for you."

"We'll stand guard out here," Jake said.

Nolan followed me into my office and watched me pull up the video. I reviewed the footage until I found where the break-in occurred. Whoever it was wore a rubber chicken mask covering their head and a bulky jacket. I wasn't sure it was a woman, but it seemed most likely, given the small build and what I thought were breasts hiding under the jacket.

I saw the robber jimmy the cash drawer open with a pry bar, then move into my office. The safe showed some damage from where the person tried to pry it open but failed. Then, as the burglar was leaving, he or she paused, walked down one of the store aisles and grabbed two bags of Mint-Os candy. The person left, and that was the end.

"It was Linda." I saved the clip and downloaded it, then copied it onto a flash drive to give to the police when they arrived.

"What makes you say that?"

"It looked like a woman and the Mint-Os. She sucks on those things obsessively."

"Can't arrest someone on candy preferences."

I leaned down to open the safe. Everything was still in place inside, as I expected. The safe seemed to function fine, despite now having several gashes around its metal door.

"It's enough to send the police in the right direction." I got up and walked back out front.

One cellophane wrapper rested on the floor in front of the broken register. The same Mint-O wrapper I'd seen Linda with, and the same kind stolen off the shelf.

I pointed to it. "More proof."

Nolan checked his watch. "The cops should be here soon."

I slid my phone from my back pocket and snapped a few photos, but there wasn't much to see.

"Good thing we only keep about a hundred bucks in there," I said. "If she had gotten into the safe, that would be a much bigger problem."

A flash of headlights drew my attention. "I bet that's Longshore and Randall."

"My two favorite cops," Nolan said.

We walked outside to greet the officers.

"This is becoming one of our regular stops," Officer Longshore said to me. He pulled his loose pants up higher on his scrawny waist. He grinned at me and stared too long.

I chuckled uncomfortably. "At least no one died this time."

Nolan shook their hands and went into cop mode as he explained all he had found at the scene.

"We'll need to talk to the witness," Officer Randall said. He, too, pulled at his belt, trying to keep his pants up over his round belly.

"Andre!" Nolan called to his friend, who stood with Jake off to the side.

"He's a witness?" I asked.

"He was the one who noticed the office door was open. He went in to see what was going on."

Randall asked Andre several questions, writing down the answers in his little notebook.

Longshore came over to take my official statement. When I finished describing the damage to the store, I gave him the flash drive. "The video footage is on here. She wore a mask, but I know it was Linda Dorsey because of the Mint-Os."

I took Longshore inside to show him the wrapper on the floor and the missing bags of candy. "She eats those things constantly. She's also threatened me more than once."

He took notes and nodded along. "Well, nothing much was stolen, so..."

"So...?" I raised my eyebrows. "So, you're not going to bother doing much or what?"

"We do have other cases to work on, miss."

"Well, this one is easy. And when I solve the new murder case, I'll let you know." I gave a curt smile.

He narrowed his eyes at me. "The murder case is not your concern."

I shrugged. "Jerry's wife had him murdered. Or did it herself. I don't have all the proof yet, but I'm working on it."

Longshore put his hands on his hips. "Now, you have been told time and again to keep out of official police business."

"There was no police business involved with me talking to Jerry's wife. She is very guilty, by the way.

Everyone thinks so. She admits she's happy he's gone. He cheated on her a lot and planned to leave her for another woman. They got into a huge fight right before his death, and that's why Jerry was in the campground in the first place. I think that provides plenty of motive, don't you?"

Longshore pushed his tongue into his cheek and squinted at me. "Hey, Randall. Come over and hear this."

Randall walked away from Andre and Nolan to join us. "What's up?"

"Our little sleuth here thinks she solved the Jerry Bishop case. Isn't that cute?"

"The goat-pen guy?" Randall asked. "They said low blood sugar did it. Might not even be murder."

Longshore nodded slowly. "Yup. But Thea thinks she can do our job better than us."

I tightened my hand into a fist. "Only because I have in the last two murders, but who's counting?"

Randall and Longshore exchanged glances.

"Submit an official statement," Longshore said, "and we'll take a look at it."

"Yeah, and *we'll* decide if it's murder and who did it," Randall added.

I wanted to roll my eyes but forced a smile instead. "I'll do that."

Longshore turned to Randall. "If you're done with the witness, we better get over to Rollie's."

"Why?" I asked. "Did something happen over there, too?"

"Police business," Longshore said at the same time Randall said, "Another break in." Longshore glared at Randall and smacked his shoulder with the back of his hand before walking off.

I looked to Nolan, who appeared to have overheard. When the cops got into their cruiser, I said, "We should check on Enid."

Andre and Jake walked back over to us.

"That was interesting," Andre said with a head shake.

"Not exactly the most competent PD," Nolan agreed.

"I'm going to call Curtis to go on patrol while we check on Enid," I said to Nolan.

"You know..." Jake looked to Andre, then me. "We were thinking that maybe we'll take shifts doing security. I'm not too sure that Curtis is... effective enough."

"If you're offering, I'll gladly accept," I said. "Curtis has been more distracted than normal lately."

"She moved in," Nolan said.

"Rose did?"

Nolan nodded and laughed. "The two of them... I see the lights on at all hours, and sometimes his camper gets rocking. Literally."

I scrunched my face in disgust. "Not a visual I needed. But I'm glad he's found someone." I turned to Jake and Andre. "If either of you want the golf cart, the keys are in my office. Feel free to help yourself to anything in the store, just leave me a list for inventory. And there's a coffeemaker in my office."

Nolan and I got into his truck. I yawned and rubbed my eyes as I pulled my seatbelt on. "Think we'll get any sleep tonight?"

"Depends how bad Rollie's is."

My stomach knotted as we drove. I hoped nothing terrible had gone down.

When we pulled in, the cop car was there, and I could see Enid talking to the officers through the large windows in the front of the store. The front door wasn't busted, and she looked tired and pale but otherwise okay.

The police wouldn't allow us past the front entry, but from there, we could see plenty. Many shelves had been disturbed, and bags of chips lay scattered across the floor. Speedy was in the far corner, hiding under a bench. I didn't see Sunny Boy, which worried me. Some boxes of food had been trampled, but I saw no shattered windows or smashed bottles or anything like that. Whoever it was hadn't been bent on destruction. Just money.

When Enid finished talking, she hurried over to us. "Are you two okay? I heard they got your store, too."

"They only got a hundred bucks and some candy." I gave her a long hug. "How are you?"

"Okay. I'd made my deposit at the bank, and they didn't go over there. Just what was in the register, and that wasn't much. We both got lucky. Some items are missing, and I'll replace my locks, but it wasn't too bad, all in all. I'm glad they didn't break the windows. Those things are darn expensive."

"What was missing?" I asked.

"Well, that part's a bit strange. They were specific. The entire inventory of Passion Perfect lipstick and Pretty Pinkalicious nail polish are gone. Just those colors." Enid shrugged.

I could see Linda wearing shades with names like that. It was also pretty unlikely that two different burglars happened to rob two stores a mile apart at the same time on the same night. "Had to be Linda. Don't you think?" I asked Nolan.

"Looks that way, but you know how these things go," he said. "Someone could be setting her up, and lots of people like Mint-Os and makeup."

"Maybe the police will actually do something about this," I said.

Enid put her hand on my shoulder. "We can only hope."

CHAPTER 12

Since the Outer Branson Police Department didn't have the best track record at solving crimes, I was shocked when I got a phone call from Officer Longshore the next day.

"We have the guilty party in custody," he said.

"Who is it?"

"Linda Dorsey. We found evidence of the missing items in her possession, as well as the mask worn during the robbery."

"Good. Guess I solved another one for you."

"We'll need you to come down and identify your stolen items and the mask."

I held back my laughter at his blatant dismissal of my words. "I'll come down as soon as I can." I hung up and picked up my walkie to call Nolan. "The police arrested Linda for the break-ins."

"Huh. Good."

"I have to go ID our property."

"You do that while I get the turtle sign back in place."

"No, no," I whined. "She's on the road again?"

"I think she's going back to the pond."

"Is the nest okay? No sign of kitten interference?"

"Not that I can see. Ricky's been poking around and left us a pile of droppings nearby, but he didn't get in, either."

"Great. I'm heading out to get this over with," I said. "Gar's in here. Where are you?"

"Cleaning out the critter pen."

"How's the memorial?" I asked.

"Tearful and busy as ever."

"I'll send Gar your way."

I left the office with Gar, and Nolan called to him when we walked outside. I drove twenty minutes to the police station and waited at the front desk. Several minutes later, Longshore walked out to greet me.

He gave a smug smile and sucked his teeth. "We have some things for you to take a look at, Miss Pagoni."

"That's why I'm here."

"Follow me."

He led me to a room in the back of the building. Several items were spread across a metal table. The room felt sterile with its dingy white walls and florescent lighting. The large window made me feel watched, though I wasn't under arrest. On the table, I spotted a torn bag of Mint-Os.

I pointed to the candy. "Those. They came from my store."

The lipstick and nail polish had to be what was missing from Rollie's. The other items looked like they had been dumped from a purse—things every woman carries: tissues, gum, headache medicine, chapstick, nail files. One item stuck out to me as curious, though. One lonely test strip, like the kind Enid used in her blood sugar tester, sat partially hidden under an old coupon for toothpaste.

"Did you find any cash?" I asked. "There was about $100 missing from the register."

Longshore shook his head. "Sorry."

At least it hadn't been more. "That's all then."

I signed my statement and left the building. As I drove home, I wondered about the test strip. Could it mean something? But what, other than Linda might have diabetes? Lots of people did, so it didn't tie her to anything related to Jerry just because he'd died of low blood sugar. Still, it stuck in my mind as more than a coincidence. It was time I went deeper into Jerry's life. Really find out who was most likely to have killed him.

I stopped at Rollie's on my way back. When I entered the store, Sunny Boy sat in front of the counter while Enid rang up a customer.

I petted the dog while I waited for Enid to finish and smiled at her customer as he walked by.

"Whew, it's been a morning." Enid covered her mouth as she yawned. "Being woken in the night like that has me all messed up today."

"I know what you mean. It's been a four-coffee kind of day." I rubbed my eyes and yawned back. "I just came from the police station. They actually solved the robbery."

"Only because you told them where to look."

I shrugged. "I'm just glad Linda is in custody. With the event being five days away, I'm worried she might show up and cause trouble if she gets out."

"I hear you don't have much cause to worry these days." Enid gave a sly grin and tilted her head.

"What do you mean?"

"I heard you have a whole trio of hot, muscular men over there, watching the place."

I laughed. "Nolan's friends are here for the week and offered to help out when the store was broken into."

Enid tapped her lip as she thought. "Does Nolan have any... older friends?"

I chuckled. "Not that I know of. Maybe ask Curtis. Rose just moved in with him."

"Ooo!" Enid's hands went into the air and vibrated in excitement. "That's some juicy news. Good for him."

"I was thinking that maybe if I interview some of Jerry's past mistresses, I can learn more about him. Can you tell me who some of them were?"

"Well, let's see." She tapped her finger against her lips. "Oh, you'll need to write these down, honey. I can think of ten off the top of my head."

"Oh." I got my notebook ready. "Start naming names."

"Monica Long, Gloria Stone, Tina Patel, Paula Holland. Two Sarahs: Johnson and Jenkins, Danielle Santiago, Tiffany Burke, Jennie Rice. Who am I forgetting? Oh! There was a Stacey Fowler and an Erin Chen."

"That's 11."

"Plus that Mandy Rogers, but you knew that."

I whistled. "He slept with this many different women?"

"He was at it a long time. Must've needed a lot of purse inspiration. And those are only the ones I know about. Probably at least that many more if you count one-night stands and hookers."

"Hookers?"

She raised a shoulder. "The man liked to have sex, I guess. And had the money for it."

I shook my head. How could this be the same weird Jerry I'd encountered in my store? Were his purses really so coveted that it outweighed his strangeness?

"This is a lot of women to talk to." I tapped my pen on the counter. "Who do you think I should start with? Who is the most recent before Mandy?"

"Gloria and then Tina."

"Are any married with an angry husband?"

"Not sure about the angry part, but the one Sarah is married. Jenkins. And then that Tiffany."

"Thanks. Jerry must've been one busy guy." I closed my notebook. "I'm going to get started on these. Do you happen to know where I can find Sarah or Tiffany?"

Enid pressed her mouth into a line and thought. "Sarah works at the clothing store beside the sandwich shop downtown. Tiffany used to work in a doctor's office, but I'm not so sure she's in the area anymore."

"I'll start downtown then." I hugged Enid goodbye and left the store.

If Jerry had such a long line of mistresses, that left a lot of options for possible suspects. Five days wasn't much time to figure out who was the most guilty. And then find the evidence to prove they did it. Barbara was still my primary choice, but I had nothing to show the police. Yet.

I pulled into the campground and grumbled when I saw the turtle sign. I drove slowly over the wooden boards beside the road and turned up to my cabin. I hadn't seen Hennie in a while, and she would know exactly which clothing store/sandwich shop combo Enid meant.

I sent her a text. "Got some new persons of interest. Want to come?"

She sent back, "And just when I was feeling bored!"

I took that to mean she would be down shortly. While I waited for her, I returned to the office to check in with Sally.

"How's it going?" I asked.

"Okay..." Sally shifted her weight and looked away.

"Something up?"

"There are some messages for you."

She hung her head and slid a stack of little square notes my way.

"I'm so sorry," Sally said. "She called yesterday and I forgot to tell you. She sounded really mad today."

The first message said, "Call Phyllis at the library." The second one was more insistent: "Call Phyllis at the library right away." Then, "Phyllis called again." And the final note: "Phyllis asks that you call her back immediately."

I smacked my forehead. I'd forgotten all about taking a bill to the library. "Thanks, Sally. It's my fault. I was supposed to do something for her and didn't."

I rummaged in my office for a minute to find a bill with my name and the campground address. It was more difficult than I thought since I paid most of the bills online. Luckily, our trash service was local and outdated, so they still had a paper-only bill. I tucked it into my purse and walked outside.

The turtle nest looked secure and the turtle still sat on the road. "You can stay at the pond, you know," I told her.

She responded by opening her jaw and snapping it shut.

I heard the hum of Hennie's four-wheeler and squinted into the sunlight to watch for her. She appeared through the trees as she rode closer.

"She's still here?" Hennie got off her four-wheeler and shook her head at the turtle. "Must be the most maternal turtle I've ever seen. She wants to guard her eggs. Isn't that sweet?"

"Yeah. It would be if she'd stay off the road."

"So, what are we digging up today?"

"One of Jerry's recent mistresses, Sarah. She works at the clothing store beside the sandwich shop downtown."

Hennie put her hand to her stomach. "We're stopping there first? They have some good roast beef."

"Sure."

We took my truck downtown and parked in front of a shop with a little sign on the front that simply read, "Sandwiches." Inside didn't look any more special than the outside. A few tables off to the right, a long counter of sandwich items, and a bored-looking teenager behind the counter.

I followed Hennie's lead and ordered the roast beef. I hadn't been expecting anything spectacular, given the appearance of the place, but when I took a bite, I was put in my place. It might have been the most juicy, flavorful roast beef sandwich I'd ever eaten in my life. Before we left, I ordered another to go. If I didn't bring Nolan one, I'd never hear the end of it.

I put the extra sandwich in my truck before we walked over to the clothing shop.

Everything the small store sold had to be ten years old. The racks were filled with high-waisted mom jeans, button-down cardigan sweaters—in the middle of the summer—and t-shirts printed with "I visited Outer Branson" that boasted 75% off clearance tags.

An eager woman approached us. If Jerry had a mistress type, she fit it. She was an attractive woman, just as Kimberly and Mandy were, with the same long hair. Her fashion style was clearly above the clothing she sold, and she looked well put together—also a recurrent feature among Jerry's ladies.

"Hi, there," she said. "What are you looking for today?"

"A woman named Sarah Jenkins," I said. "Is that you by any chance?"

The woman's eyes widened, and she slid her hand over her name tag. I thought I saw an S just before her finger covered it. "Who wants to know?" Her eyes darted from Hennie to me.

I glanced at Hennie. We hadn't had much of a plan for how to approach this.

"We... wanted to let you know... that you won," Hennie said.

"Won what?"

"My giveaway." Hennie nodded once and smiled.

"Oh. I didn't know I entered a giveaway." The woman looked at us for a moment. "So, where is the prize?"

"Uhh..." Hennie looked back to me.

I jumped to action. "There's actually a whole line of Hennie's Honey products, and the choice is up to you which product you receive."

The woman nodded and finally dropped her hand to reveal the "Sarah" on her little blue tag.

"You can pick from bottled honey, face soap, or lotion," Hennie said.

Sarah rubbed her hands together. "I can always use a good lotion."

"Great." Hennie clapped and jerked her thumb toward the door. "I'll just run and grab it."

Hennie walked out to my truck, and I blinked after her. We hadn't brought any sort of products with us, so what in the world was she doing?

"So... do you like working here?" I asked.

"It's okay. I've been here a long time. But there's not much else in Outer Branson."

I nodded. "I own the campground."

Her eyes flared. "The one where..."

I gave a sad smile and nodded. "Did you know Jerry Bishop?" At least the murder made for an easy transition into questioning.

Sarah looked to the side and scratched her elbow. "I guess you could say that. Though no one was supposed to know."

"Ahh. I've heard that Jerry liked to have secret flings."

"Yeah." She rolled her eyes. "Lots."

"Did you date him for a long time?"

"I wouldn't call what we did 'dating' but it went on a few months. Until he met Mandy."

"Did he name a purse after you?"

She beamed and nodded. "The 'Lynn'—my middle name. We couldn't use my first name because there already was a 'Sarah' and because, like I said, he wanted to keep it a secret. Do you want to see my purse?" She scampered away before I could say no.

When Sarah returned a moment later, she proudly held out the black leather triangular purse with a large, three-dimensional, red leather flower on the front.

"It's nice," I lied.

Sarah gazed adoringly at the purse and traced the edges of the leather flower with her fingertip.

"Did Jerry stay loyal to Mandy?" I asked. "Is that why you stopped seeing him when he met her?"

"No," Sarah said. "But I saw him less since he gave so much time to Mandy. I got fed up and cut it off totally a few months ago."

"I don't blame you. Were you jealous over Mandy?"

Sarah shrugged. "Not really. I was never the only one he was with, so how could I be?"

She didn't seem angry or vengeful at all. Either she was a really good liar, or she was over Jerry. I glanced at her hand and saw the ring. "Were you married at the time?"

Sarah said, "He knows. My husband. We've always had an open marriage. Not my choice, but it has its perks sometimes."

Interesting. "Then he wasn't mad about Jerry?"

"Why would he be?"

Not that I was a marriage expert, but I didn't see how that could lead to a healthy home life. "Did you ever meet any of Jerry's other ladies?"

"I've seen Mandy in town a few times, but we never talked. He dated my friend Kimmy, but that was back in high school."

My heart leapt at the name. "Kimmy? *Kimmy Cakes* Kimmy?"

Sarah smiled. "Yeah, that's her bakery. She makes amazing cupcakes."

"I've had them. I didn't know she dated Jerry." In fact, Kimberly had said she didn't know Jerry at all.

"Like I said, it was back in high school. Though..." Sarah gave a quick look around before continuing. "He was pretty mean to her, and I know Kimmy was heartbroken. I wouldn't be surprised if she tried to get back together with him later."

"After twenty years, she was still interested in him?" Kimmy and Jerry had to be in their thirties, like me.

"I think she wanted revenge. Jerry was just starting out with the purses, and she never got one named after her, even though she put up with all the long hours he spent drawing and sewing the prototypes. She swears the 'Karla' is really her purse, but that Jerry changed the name from Kimmy after they broke up. He was so harsh about it all." Sarah shook her head. "Kimmy is super sweet until you cross her. I made that mistake one time. Oh, but don't tell her I told you any of this. She'd be pissed."

"No, I won't. You think she had a plan to get back at Jerry?" This was turning out to be quite a fruitful interview. What was Hennie doing still out in the truck?

"Kimmy never said anything like that, but I wonder."

"What did he do that was so mean?"

Sarah laughed humorlessly. "It was like something out of *Carrie*, I swear."

An image of Kimberly covered in blood came to my mind. Surely she didn't mean Jerry had done something that terrible.

"It was right in the middle of the senior prom. Kimmy thought they might get married a few years after high school. Like when she finished culinary school. But Jerry had other plans. During the last song, when it was all quiet and everyone was dancing, he stepped back from her, and said really loud, 'I can't stand you anymore. You're stupid and immature. I'm done.' He stormed off, and everyone watched as Kimmy just stood there and burst into tears. She told me later that right before that, she was trying to convince him that they should have kids. Guess he didn't want any."

"Wow." Not quite as horrific as *Carrie*, but highly embarrassing nonetheless. "Do you think she would have actually killed him, though? Over that?"

"Probably not. But besides his wife, Kimmy is the only other person I know who has something against Jerry. He never did anything like that to me."

"Why did you have a relationship with him after what he did to your friend?"

Sarah blushed and smiled to herself. "He and Kimmy were a long time ago, and I wanted my own purse. Plus, I had to see if what everyone says about him was true."

Not this again. "Ahh. I've heard rumors about him in the bedroom."

"They're not just rumors." Sarah kept smiling and played with her necklace.

"Well, I guess I better let you get back to work."

"Nice chatting with you," she said.

I held up a hand as I walked toward the door.

"Hey!" Sarah shouted after me. "Where's my lotion?"

I ran for the truck and hopped in, then pulled away as fast as I could. I looked over at Hennie. "Nice plan you had there. What were you doing while I was in there?"

"Giving you time to talk to her."

"She wants her lotion."

Hennie flicked a hand toward the shop. "Maybe we made a mistake. She said she never entered. We might've confused her with Sarah Johnson."

"I found out some good stuff. But we better get this bill over to Phyllis before we go see about it."

As I drove, I told her what Sarah said about Kimberly.

Hennie pointed out, "You said Kimberly was acting shifty."

"Maybe she's not as cute and innocent as she comes off. I thought we could talk to her again next."

"If we survive Phyllis."

CHAPTER 13

I had my apologetic smile in place before I even stepped inside the library. I brandished my bill in my hand so Phyllis could see right away that I'd come to fulfill my promise.

When we neared the counter, Phyllis stood and crossed her arms. "You promised, Thea. And then you didn't come."

"I know, and I am so sorry. My store was broken into and I was up all night, and it's been really, really hard." She didn't need to know the break in happened *after* I was meant to have brought in the bill.

Her face softened slightly, but she looked to Hennie for confirmation.

"It was awful." Hennie shook her head with a sad expression. "They got Rollie's, too. Poor Enid. Almost had a heart attack."

Phyllis sucked in a breath and put her hand to her chest. "I had no idea. Is she okay?"

"We're all recovering," I said. "And here's the bill. So sorry again that I didn't bring it yesterday."

"Well, I can understand." She offered a sympathetic smile as she took the paper. "I'll just make a copy of this and you can be on your way. I do appreciate you coming all the way down here to bring it in. Gotta have our files complete, you know that."

"Of course."

She finished at the copier and handed my bill back. "Did you find out anything more about the killer?"

"Still working on it," I said.

"You let me know, now, if you discover something," she warned. "I want to be the first!"

I gave her a thumbs up. "I'll try."

Phyllis chuckled and pointed at me. "Don't you try, you just do it now, you hear?"

I nodded and backed away from the counter. "I will. Thanks. And sorry again!"

I hurried out of the library with Hennie on my heels.

"At least she wasn't too mad," I said as I slid back into the driver's seat.

Hennie shook her head and *tsk*ed at me. "You know what you just did? If you don't tell her something, you'll bring on the wrath of the Outer Branson Library."

"Do they throw books or something?"

"They might."

We pulled into Kimmy Cakes, and when we entered the shop, again, I was overwhelmed by the amount of sweetness in the air. Maybe it was all the sugar that made Kimberly so peppy.

She came to greet us as we approached the counter. "Welcome back!"

I smiled. "We really loved the cupcakes we tried. They're going to make the event great."

"I second that," Hennie added.

"We do have one little problem, though," I said.

"Oh? What's that?" Kimberly's bottom lip stuck out in a slight pout.

"If we don't get this case resolved, the whole event might be ruined. When there's an unsolved murder going on, people tend to cancel their reservations."

Kimberly pulled her eyebrows together and nodded. "That sounds bad. What will you do?"

"Hope that the police figure things out," I said.

Hennie harrumphed. "And they ain't so far."

Kimberly shook her head. "Poor Jerry. He could've lived a long, happy life. Who knows how many more purses he might've designed."

She seemed to get lost in thought, and I wondered if her mind drifted back to her high school days.

"I'm not sure how I can help, though," she said after several moments.

"You said before that you didn't know Jerry." I gulped and blurted out, "But I know that you not only knew him, you dated him. And he hurt you. Badly."

Kimberly's cheerfulness vanished. "So what if he did?" she snapped.

"Why did you lie?"

"Wouldn't you? I didn't want to look guilty, having been the girl he dumped in front of the entire school." Clearly her bitterness hadn't faded with time.

"Except that lying about it actually makes you look more guilty," I said. "Innocent people don't hide things."

She glared at me. "Do you think I would ruin all of what I've built over him? He's not worth it. And I don't need people poking around my business, making it seem like I might've committed murder."

The door swung open, and a mom with her young son entered the shop. Kimberly smiled, waved to them, and then hissed at me, "Shush."

She scurried over to help her customers. I raised my eyebrows at Hennie.

"Interesting," Hennie said.

"To say the least."

When the customers left, Kimberly came back to us.

"Look, I don't know what else I can say to you. I'm over Jerry. Way over. I didn't have anything to do with his death. But if I had to guess, I'd bet that wife of his finally got sick of all his wandering ways. I wouldn't put up with that. No way." Then she put a hand on her hip.

"Does this have anything to do with you getting into my backroom the other day? What did you do back there?" She glared at Hennie.

"That was an innocent mistake." Hennie held up her hands.

Kimberly curled her lip back and glared harder. Her expression made my insides squirm. Time to get out.

"If that's all," I said, "then when did you say you needed the final payment for the cupcakes?"

She turned her cold stare at me. "Day before the event. Just like it says on your contract. They won't be delivered if it's not paid."

"Got it. Thanks!"

Hennie and I left the shop and took off in my truck.

"Did she seem over Jerry to you?" I asked.

"Nope."

"Didn't think so. Sarah said she might've tried to rekindle things. I wonder if anyone saw them together."

"For Kimmy's sake, I hope not. Paranoid little thing."

"I know. But is she paranoid because she's guilty or because she's just that high strung?"

"Could go either way."

When we pulled into the campground, Hennie put her hand on my shoulder. "Thanks for the sleuthing. I gotta get home. Expecting a shipment of beets from the family farm in Pennsylvania. Can't miss it!" She rubbed her hands together vigorously.

"Beets? What are you going to do with those?"

She grinned. "I like to make a nice big batch of beet wine for the fall."

I couldn't think of anything more disgusting, so I nodded and gave a weak smile. "I'm off to deliver this." I patted the bag sitting between us on the seat.

Hennie saluted me, then hopped out of my truck. I drove slowly through the campground, keeping my eyes peeled.

I found Nolan clearing large brush from a few sites in the main loop. Gar retrieved sticks and set them in a somewhat tidy pile. I hopped out of my truck, bagged sandwich in hand, and walked to them.

"Did you train him to do that?" I pointed to Gar's pile as I rubbed his head hello.

Nolan gave me a half smile. "Good trick, eh?"

"Yeah. Free labor." I held out the bag. "Hennie and I went into town. You don't happen to like roast beef sandwiches, do you? We went to this place—"

"That sandwich shop downtown?" He yanked the bag from me and tore open the wrapper. "You know how I feel about sandwiches." He took a deep sniff of the bread and sighed contently. Then he took a huge bite and chewed, a smile plastered on his face. "Best roast beef in all of Missouri," he said with a full mouth.

"I thought you might like it." I chuckled as he took another huge bite. "So, we talked to a few people today."

He nodded and chewed. Gar hopped away to find another stick for his pile. "Kimberly might not be too innocent after all. She not only dated Jerry, but was dumped by him in a quite public and demeaning way. And she's not exactly over it."

I repeated the things Enid had told me and gave all the details from my conversations with Sarah and Kimberly.

"What are your leads?" Nolan asked between final bites.

"Not sure. I have nothing on Kimberly except her lies and reaction. Same thing with Barbara. There's no evidence pointing to anyone."

"You could see if Mandy has anything to say about Kimberly."

"Yeah." I glanced behind him to the campsite. "Is there a lot left to do? We have a bunch of people arriving tomorrow."

"That's why I'm out here. These sites get left for last usually, but we're going to have close to half capacity."

I sighed. "I keep thinking at some point, half capacity isn't going to be our best hope."

He balled the sandwich wrapper and tossed it into a black trash bag nearby. When it landed, Gar pounced on it, then ran off to search out another stick.

"That was exactly what I needed. Thanks." Nolan gave me a quick hug and kiss. "You do know how to keep a man happy."

I chuckled. "I try."

"It's getting better," he assured me. "Despite all these deaths, people are coming, and it's somehow getting the word out. Everyone knows about Cedar Fish."

"Then where are they all?"

He stuck out his lower jaw and did his best *Godfather* impression. "Waiting for you to make them an offer they can't refuse."

I rolled my eyes, but laughed. "I'll get to work on that."

CHAPTER 14

The new cash drawer arrived by way of a shiny, white FedEx van. I read through the directions in the box and set up the new drawer. We'd been using an old, metal lockbox for cash in the meantime, and it wasn't the most efficient method. I hadn't found anything safer than a deadbolt for the front door, but after Nolan changed the locks yesterday and added a second deadbolt, I figured there wasn't much else to be done. The safe had held, so that was a good sign. With the cameras in place, we were as break-in proof as we could realistically be.

Since both of my sidekicks were busy, I headed out on my own to talk to Mandy. Luckily, I'd been thinking ahead when Mandy checked out and had gotten her home address under the excuse that the police might need to contact her. I plugged the address into my GPS on my phone and followed the directions to a small townhouse in a rural area.

The place was neither well-kept nor neglected. The yard had been recently mowed, but the flower beds were full of weeds. A Fourth of July wreath hung on the door, but the windows beside the door appeared grungy.

I knocked and gave a sad smile when Mandy answered. Only then did I think that I should have brought her something. Flowers or chocolates or some other sympathy gift. Too late now.

"Hey," I said softly. "How are you?"

She sucked in a slow breath. "Okay."

I shifted my weight and felt the panic rise. Why had I come so unprepared? I needed Hennie or Nolan to balance out my awkwardness. "Have you... gotten things settled?"

She wrapped her arms around her waist. "I guess? I'm trying to adjust."

"How was the funeral?" Was that even an appropriate question to ask?

"I didn't, umm, go actually." She blushed and looked down to pick at the hem of her shirt.

"I guess it would have been hard with his wife there."

"And his whole family hates me."

"That's hard. You have enough going on right now."

She let out a shaky sigh. "Yeah."

"It's too bad Barbara couldn't put aside her issues to let you say goodbye."

Mandy lifted a shoulder. "I didn't even try. Things haven't been good with her, and I thought it might not be the best time to try to be friends, you know?"

I nodded. "Has she ever threatened you or anything? Made you feel afraid?"

"Lots of times. I used to get a text or a call every week."

"Really? Do the police know that?"

Mandy nodded. "They didn't seem to think it was important."

I rolled my eyes. "The more I find out about Barbara, the more I think she's guilty."

"But if she wasn't there..."

"That's what I can't figure out. She must've found a way to poison him. Something that maybe takes a few days to work? Was he feeling ill earlier that day?"

"Not that I remember. But there is something..." She pulled her arms tighter around her middle. "Well, I don't know for sure if it's anything."

"If what's anything?"

She glanced around. "Do you want to come in?"

"I'd love to."

I followed her into a semi-clean room. Much like the outside, I saw evidence of a well lived-in home. The clutter was mostly reserved to corners and a few surfaces. The floor looked to be recently vacuumed, but there was visible dust on the photo frames. Probably about what my cabin looked like. I didn't have much time to deep clean.

"I want to show you something," Mandy said.

I sat on the sofa and waited for her to return. In the meantime, I looked around to make sure nothing suspicious jumped out at me.

When Mandy returned, she carried a small tin. "Barbara gave me this."

The tin was bare aluminum except for a handwritten label stuck to the top. The label read, "Bishop Friendship Tea."

"She gave you this?" I couldn't help feeling shocked by such a seemingly kind gesture. That shock quickly turned to suspicion.

"One time she threatened to kill me. Usually, she says she'll tell my family or my boss or something like that. But once she actually said I should watch my back because she would be lurking in the shadows."

"Whoa."

"Yeah." Mandy shivered. "Then the next day, she showed up on my doorstep with flowers and that tin of tea. I was afraid to drink it."

"I would be, too. Mind if I take it?"

"I'm never going to drink it. I think I kept it just in case. If she ever did anything, I thought I could give it to the police to check."

"My friend has a poison test kit. I'd like to test the tea and see what it reveals."

Mandy nodded. "Let me know if you find something. I'd like to think she was being sincere, but I can't see why she'd suddenly do something nice."

"And she called it 'friendship tea' and used her last name. Almost like she wanted to send a message."

"I guess I didn't get it." Mandy's mouth fell into a slight smirk.

"What about Kimberly Henson? Do you know her?"

Mandy huffed and crossed her arms. "Yes. Unfortunately."

"Did she cause trouble for you?"

"Who hasn't?" Mandy threw her hands up and let them fall hard. "She wanted Jerry back. I don't blame her, but he dumped her like twenty years ago! Get over it already." She shook her head and sneered.

"What did she do?"

"She would show up at his work or call him or send him messages. She couldn't accept that he'd moved on forever. It was a little pathetic, actually. She even has photos of the two of them from high school on her on-line profile."

"Does she really?" Kimberly made herself look more and more guilty as the days went on. "Did she ever contact you?"

"No. Thank goodness. One crazy woman is all I can handle. I don't know what will happen in a few months."

I raised an eyebrow. "A few months?"

She dropped her hand to her stomach. "When the baby comes, Barbara might freak out. I'm sure Jerry's family is going to want to know this baby. He doesn't have any other kids. She'll hate that." A slight smile formed on her lips. Barbara and Kimberly weren't the only ones who sought revenge, apparently.

"Congratulations. I had no idea."

"Not many people do. But that's what made Jerry decide to leave Barbara. He never would have otherwise."

Jerry must've changed his no-kids stance from the Kimberly days. Or maybe he just hadn't wanted them with Kimberly.

"Seems like that might've pushed Barbara over the edge," I said.

Mandy nodded. "It might've."

"Do you think Kimberly could have killed him when she realized she couldn't get him back?"

Mandy thought a moment. "I guess. Hey, do you think this could be on *Forensic Files*? Like, I maybe could be on there and get famous?"

"Uhh... I don't think they still make that show."

"Oh." She shrugged.

"And who knows if the killer will ever be caught."

"No one hated Jerry as much as his wife did. Not even Kimberly," Mandy said. "That much I know for sure."

I nodded. "Most women seemed to like him quite a lot."

"He was a likable guy."

I couldn't agree, but I wouldn't dare put down the dead to someone who'd loved him. "I wish I'd gotten to know him better."

Mandy looked around uncomfortably. It felt like time to go.

I held the tin up. "Besides this, is there anything you know of that could prove Barbara did it?"

"I kept all the messages she sent me."

"Could I see them?"

Mandy took her phone from her pocket and tapped it a few times before handing it to me. I looked over the texts. Most said things like, "Stay away from my husband, you tramp," or "I will ruin your life, hussie." Nothing life threatening, but still indicative of the type of person Barbara was.

"Thanks for showing me these." I handed the phone back. "I'll let you know if we find anything in the tea." I got to my feet.

Mandy stood with me. "If there's anything else I can do, let me know. I'd love to see Barbara pay for what she did."

I said goodbye and walked out to my truck, replaying the conversation in my head. Mandy came off a lot more vengeful than I'd picked up on before, but only toward Barbara. If Barbara had been killed, Mandy would be the prime suspect. But Mandy seemed plenty innocent when it came to Jerry's death.

Before I drove off, I sent a text to Hennie. "When you're done with the beets, bring that poison test kit. I have tea that Barbara gave Mandy as an apology after threatening to kill her."

As I neared the campground, I saw taillights ahead and sensed chaos. Cedar Hollow Road never had much traffic.

The line wasn't long, but two cars waited in the campground entrance while another sat in the road, waiting to turn in. I put my hazard lights on and jumped out of my truck. I walked up to the man driving the car in front of me. His wife sat beside him and two small kids fought over a stuffed animal in the backseat. The man's muscular build and serious expression made me think he was probably one of our vets, here for the event.

"Hi there," I said, waving to the family. "You can pull into the parking lot so you're not on the road."

I pointed to where Linda had made the ruts in the grass. If the damage was already there, why not use it for my benefit?

"Yes, ma'am," he said.

I got back in my truck as he drove through the grass into the parking lot. I followed him and hopped out of my truck to a busy scene. Several people congregated outside the store, talking and drinking sodas. A couple sat on the porch swing, and a little girl had Ash on her lap, petting him and grinning ear-to-ear. Ash purred and looked like he was in heaven. Across the road, Jerry's memorial was hopping with visitors, and the candles and flowers now stretched around a second side of the fence.

My heart warmed at the sight of the busyness. This was closer to how I remembered the campground. Full of people. Things going on. Laughter and fun and a little chaos. This was how it should be.

My smile faltered when I entered the office. Sally looked distressed, and Curtis was nowhere in sight. A line at the front counter was four people deep.

I set the tin of tea under the counter and pushed up my sleeves. "Who's checking in?" I took out a stack of forms, wishing, not for the first time, that we had a better way to do all of this. If I didn't find a software soon that made Sally's job easier, I'd have to hire a second employee to handle the volume as our reservations went up. Assuming they continued to go up.

Hennie walked in as I handed out pens to the waiting campers. She gawked at the line and stared blankly at me.

I gave her a sheepish grin and asked, "Could you help a minute?"

She nodded and stood behind the register. A camper handed her two cold drinks and a box of trash bags. Hennie took them and turned to me. "How do I ring these up?"

"Why don't you help get people checked in and I'll ring?"

Hennie nodded and switched places with me. I rang my camper up as fast as I could and sucked in a slow breath of patience while I waited for him to fish change from his pocket.

When we'd cleared the rush of people, I let out a deep sigh and held up my hand to high-five Hennie and Sally. "Good teamwork, ladies."

Sally pushed her hair back and said, "Whew. That was rough."

"It's good to see so many people here," I said. Several shoppers still roamed the store.

"I'm ready for testing," Hennie said.

"Right." I grabbed the tea tin and said to Sally, "Call me if it gets nuts again."

We went into my office. I pushed papers out of the way to clear a spot for us to work.

Hennie lifted the aluminum lid and sniffed the tea. "Kinda musty."

"What does that mean?"

"Might just be old, but water hemlock has a musty sorta smell."

My heart skipped. Could Barbara really have tried to poison Mandy?

Hennie took a few pinches of the tea and sprinkled them in the glass container of the kit. She added a drizzle of water and stirred. Then she dipped one of the test strips into the mixture and set it on my desk.

"Whoa." Hennie snatched the strip up and inspected it. "Look!"

The test square had changed color to a dark purple.

Hennie opened the results chart and read it, then shouted with her hands in the air. "It's poison! It's poison!"

"Shh!"

I grabbed the chart from her and looked over the color icons. Next to the purple square, the definition said, "Presence of plant-based toxin detected = cicutoxin."

"Is that water hemlock?" I asked.

"You bet your boots." Hennie danced around the tiny office. "We found the killer!"

"So, Barbara really tried to kill Mandy..." My mind worked overtime. If she'd done it once, what would stop her from doing it again?

"Let's go tell them coppers that we solved the murder!" Hennie moved to the door.

"Umm, one little problem."

"What?"

"Barbara gave this tea to Mandy, not Jerry. And Mandy's alive and fine."

"Oh. Right."

"Barbara might still be the killer, but this isn't proof of Jerry's murder. We need backup on this one." I picked up the walkie talkie and asked Nolan, "You terribly busy?"

"Ehh? Kind of?" Nolan said. "What's up?"

"When I talked to Mandy, she gave me a tin of tea that Barbara had given her. I had Hennie test it, and it came back positive for the water hemlock toxin."

"Huh," he said. "Give me a minute."

"We should practice some self-defense while we're waiting." Hennie slid her feet into fighting stance and put up her fists.

"There's no room in here."

I sat at the table desk against the wall and Hennie stood beside me. We only had a few feet to spare.

"Then we'll practice close-up moves." She reached down and put her arm around my neck, pressing her forearm into my throat from behind.

I elbowed her in the side and threw a back knuckle—not connecting hard with any of my moves. I twisted and jumped to my feet to break the connection of her hold. From my new position, I punched her stomach.

Just as I threw a punch toward Hennie's nose, Nolan appeared in the doorway. He leaned against the frame with a grin. "Now that's what I call a girl fight."

Hennie and I bowed to each other and turned our attention to him.

"Look." I thrust the kit's chart at him and then pointed to the purple strip.

Nolan took a moment to look things over. "How accurate is this kit?"

"Top of the line," Hennie said with her chin high.

Nolan pressed his lips together. "You shouldn't have this. Mandy should have called the cops if she thought something was up. Now you've messed with evidence."

"There's still plenty of tea in there," I protested. "They don't have to know we did anything."

"No, you have to call them and tell them. This isn't evidence for Jerry's death, but it sets a precedent for the top suspect. It could be a problem that you brought it here. It's probably not admissible evidence now."

"It still shows Barbara's capable, though," I said.

"It shows a lot," he agreed. "But you're getting sloppy. How many times have I told you not to break any laws when you go sleuthing?"

I gulped, and a rock of guilt stuck in my throat. He could never know that Hennie and I trespassed in Barbara's yard and found water hemlock growing there. We'd have to trust that the police would find it without us pointing it out.

"Am I going to be in trouble if I call the cops?" I asked.

"Call them. Tell them what you told me about going to visit Mandy—to give condolences only—and that she gave you that. You had Hennie test it and then called them immediately when you saw the strip."

"Okay."

He shook his head and rubbed his beard. "Some days it feels like I never left the force."

I hung my head and my cheeks warmed.

He stepped forward to kiss my forehead, then turned and walked out.

Hennie whistled. "He's got it bad for you."

I raised an eyebrow at her. "What makes you say that? I just made him mad."

"Oh honey, that's not anger. You put yourself in danger and you scared him. That's how much he loves you."

"Shh!" I swatted her arm. "Don't say the 'L' word. We're not saying that. We're not in love."

Hennie laughed once and patted my shoulder. "Sure, sure."

"We're not," I insisted. "It's casual. Neither of us is looking for something like that."

"I've said it before. Just because you ain't looking, doesn't mean you ain't found it."

I picked up my phone to change the subject. I was starting to feel squirmy, like things were slipping out of my control and unraveling around me. "I need to take care of this."

Hennie sat back and put her foot on her knee.

I dialed the Outer Branson Police Department and waited on hold.

"Yes, hello," I said when the dispatcher finally returned. "I need to talk to Officer Longshore or Randall about a possible poisoning."

"Did you call Poison Control?" the woman asked.

"No one has actually been poisoned. Well, except for one person possibly, but he's already dead and won't be helped by Poison Control."

There was a pause and then, "Hold please."

I tapped my fingers on the desk until the line clicked again. "Officer Randall."

"Thea Pagoni. I have a situation I think you'll want to take a look at. It turns out that Jerry's wife tried to poison his girlfriend."

"Uh huh. How so?"

"She gave her tea that contains what we think is water hemlock, which is poisonous if consumed."

"Uh huh," he said. "Is she hurt?"

"Well no. Mandy didn't drink the tea, she gave it to me."

"Was she trying to poison you?"

"No." I growled in exasperation. "Mandy showed me the tea that Barbara gave her and then Mandy gave me the tea so I could have my friend test it."

"Did your friend drink the tea?"

"No, she used a poison detection kit."

"I see."

I waited for several moments, but he didn't continue. "I thought you guys might want to look into this since Jerry died kind of mysteriously and his wife had plenty of motive to kill him?"

"There was that insulin spike..." Randall said.

"The what?"

"The early autopsy. Never mind. I'll tell Longshore and we'll come by later."

"Okay. Thanks."

I hung up and turned to Hennie with a confused look. "I think Randall just accidentally gave me information. He said the early autopsy showed an insulin spike."

Hennie narrowed her eyes. "A big dose of insulin would drop a man's blood sugar and kill him. But how'd Jerry get dosed?"

"Diabetes is fairly common. Lots of people have access to insulin."

"Looks like our suspect list just grew."

"I sure hope it was Barbara. If it wasn't, we have a lot more work to do."

CHAPTER 15

The Outer Branson PD arrived only 20 minutes after my call. And it wasn't just one car that pulled in, but two. They parked on the side of the main entrance near the goat pen, their lights flashing over the memorial and its worried-looking visitors.

I walked out to meet them. "What's all this?" I asked Officer Longshore when he was in hearing range.

"We need to go over the scene one more time with homicide."

"Is this because of the tea and the insulin spike the autopsy showed?"

Longshore narrowed his eyes. "How do you know about that?"

"Randall mentioned something about the preliminary results."

Longshore shook his head. "You're already too involved. Now you have alleged proof of a poisoning?"

"*Attempted* poisoning. Barbara Bishop. You know, Jerry's wife who got cheated on over and over again? She gave poisoned tea to Mandy, Jerry's girlfriend. I'd guess that she poisoned Jerry, too. She must've given him insulin somehow, and it dropped his blood sugar."

"We'll be the ones deciding all that. You just answer our questions and keep your pretty little nose out of our business."

I narrowed my eyes at him. "Right." If I did that, nothing would get solved in this town. "Would you like to see the tea?"

He looked over his shoulder for Officer Randall. Randall pushed himself out of the police cruiser and made his way to us.

"Let's check out this tea claim," Longshore told him.

I took them into the office and went over the details of my conversation with Mandy, then showed them the test kit and explained how it worked.

"Do you have any evidence of Mandy's whereabouts on the day of the murder?" Longshore asked.

"She said she was at her campsite," I said. "She's not on camera anywhere near the wildlife area. No one was around Jerry when he died."

"Is she on camera at her site?" Longshore asked.

"We don't have a camera over there."

"Who was around Jerry right before he died?" Randall asked.

"Several people. He came into the store a few times. I rang him up. Other customers were in and out."

"Sounds like you were one of the last to see him alive." Longshore pushed his eyebrows up his forehead and leaned toward me.

I leaned away. "I guess I was."

"That makes the third murder in this campground this summer," Longshore went on. "And they all started the day you arrived."

"The day after I arrived, but who's keeping track?" I said. "It's been pretty terrible."

"Or pretty convenient if you're the real killer." Randall crossed his arms over his chest.

"You were the ones who put two people in jail for the other murders. If I'm the real killer and they weren't, then you have a huge problem on your hands."

The grin melted off Randall's mouth. "Well, it's suspicious timing, don't you think?"

I shrugged. "That's life. But since I've helped solve all the murders and two break-ins so far, I'd say it's good timing. And by the way, I'd look into Kimberly Henson, too. She had a grudge against Jerry and wanted him back. And she seems a little too worried about being a possible suspect."

Longshore made a note. "We have several persons of interest to talk to."

I nodded and tried to keep the sarcasm from my voice. "Sure. I trust you guys to do your job well and catch the killer fast."

Longshore and Randall left my office, and I walked out after them, pausing by Hennie, who waited near the register.

The door closed behind the officers, and she shook her head. "Those two couldn't catch a cold between them."

"I know. I want to keep an eye on them."

We walked outside as Randall and Longshore went to join the other officers at the scene. Detective Hooley had come from the city to help, so they must be getting serious about it, but they drew too much attention. Along with the ever-present fan club, a second loose crowd stood watching the lights. It didn't help that the new turtle attraction was taking place on the road just beside the flashing cop cars. Or that the memorial seemed to be quite busy today.

"Seems you got a gathering going on," Hennie said.

I took my walkie from where I'd clipped it onto my jeans' pocket. "Hey Nolan, Curtis. I think you might want to come to the main entrance. We have cops up here making a scene, and people are gathering."

As I stood there, a woman near the goat pen suddenly cried out, "Oh, Jerry!" Several ladies immediately surrounded her and covered her with hugs, but they were getting loud about their grief.

A man standing a few feet away saw me and walked over. His family trailed behind. "What's going on?"

"The cops are just searching the area," I said.

"Searching? For what exactly? And what's with...?" He waved toward the sobbing women.

"We had an unfortunate incident here a few days ago. Locals have been showing their support. Some more investigation needs to be done."

The man's wife stood beside him and pulled her two small girls close. "What does that mean? Is it safe here?"

"We do our best to make it as safe as possible. We have a security team and cameras." I looked down the road hopefully, but there was no sign of Nolan or Curtis yet.

The family wandered closer to the wildlife area to watch.

"Let's just hope a news van don't show up," Hennie said.

Nolan's truck roared into view, and I felt some tension melt from my shoulders. I walked over to meet him as he parked.

"Can you do some ex-cop magic and get them to turn off their lights? A crowd is forming, and I've already had one questioning family."

Nolan got out of the truck. "Sure. Why are they here?"

Gar jumped down from the seat, and I held onto his collar. He'd get over-excited from so many unfamiliar people to sniff at once.

"I called them about the tea," I said. "They're combing the scene again."

"They'll find a lot five days after the fact. And anything that might've been there is now either trampled or covered with flowers." He shook his head. "You told them everything?"

I nodded. Everything that wasn't illegal.

Nolan walked over to where the officers were talking by the entrance to the goat pen. Gar tried to break free of my hold, so I rubbed his head to distract him. After a few moments, an officer approached the cruisers and stopped the lights.

Good, but it didn't seem to dissuade the crowd. A family that had just checked in walked out of the office and wandered over to a group of three families watching the police. In the time it took Nolan to walk back over to us, two more groups had joined the gathering.

"What do we do about this?" I gestured to the spectators and looked to Hennie and Nolan. "Should we shut down the memorial for the night? Or for good? I don't think it's helping business."

"I don't think you should shut it down completely," Nolan said. "That might be worse. The cops should be done soon."

As we stood there, a woman broke off from the crowd and walked over. "Excuse me. You're the owner, aren't you?"

I nodded and put one hand out. Gar whined and pulled against my other. "Thea Pagoni."

"People are saying there was a murder." She shook my hand and looked over at the police cars and memorial with wide eyes. "Is that true?"

I gulped. "I'm afraid it is true. It was several days ago, and the police are checking the scene again."

The woman nodded and walked back to the crowd. A minute later, I saw her point at me as she talked loudly.

"I have a feeling this will be bad," I said.

Three men broke away next and came to us. Nolan stepped forward as they approached.

"Hi there." He shook their hands. "I'm Nolan Cade, head of security here. I hope you're enjoying your stay."

"What's this we hear about a murder?" a man in a blue shirt asked.

Nolan held his hands up. "It's true, I'm sorry to say. But everything is under control. It was a domestic situation, so nothing to fear."

The man standing in the middle spoke up next. "This was supposed to be a safe place. A safe event. It doesn't feel too safe with murders going on."

The last man added, "I don't like it one bit. I came out here to escape all this."

"I understand," Nolan said. "You have valid points, and I hear your concern. But I can assure you that the police are almost finished, and they have a solid lead." He leaned in and dropped his voice. "The guy was a cheater and his wife took revenge. You know how these things go."

The men nodded and seemed to accept this explanation.

"We have security and cameras," Nolan added. "Not to mention a campground full of vets."

The men nodded more enthusiastically, and one of them said, "Army, four years."

Nolan added, "Marine for two."

They broke into a short chat about their time serving. Nolan came back to me as the men returned to the crowd. Before Nolan even reached me, the gathering started to disperse.

"Wow. That was impressive." Seeing him in action like that had unexpectedly made me warm all over.

I hugged him and kissed his cheek.

Curtis zoomed into view on his golf cart. The top of his uniform was unbuttoned, and he wore a goofy grin under his backward hat. Rose was at his side and had curled into him, clinging to his arm while wearing her own beaming smile.

"Guess we know why it took Curtis so long to get down here," I said.

Hennie smacked me on the back. "Everyone is getting some around here except you. Better fix that!"

I closed my eyes and tried to ignore her comment. I hoped Nolan would do the same.

"What do you want Curtis to do?" I asked Nolan, grateful for a solid reason to change the subject.

"I'll hang out up here and monitor the fan club," Nolan said. "He can patrol and make sure that crowds aren't gathering in other parts. I'll talk to him."

Nolan pulled a leash from his back pocket, then clipped it on Gar's collar. I gave him one final head rub before he trotted off with Nolan.

When they walked out of earshot, I spun on my heels and put my hands on my hips. "You cannot say things like that!" I snapped at Hennie. My cheeks still burned.

"Sorry, but it's true. Don't know what you're waiting for."

"Our relationship is casual. I've told you this. Neither of us is ready for a commitment."

"Who said anything about all that?" She shook her head. "You can casually date and casually sleep together. That's one of the perks of having no strings! It's what I do."

"I'm glad that you're still... active. But I'm just not ready to go there."

"I think it'd help with your stress. You keep chewing on ice like you do and you'll end up chipping your teeth."

I had already. Twice. "Maybe someday. For now, I'll just... take up yoga or something."

"Yeah." Hennie rolled her eyes. "That usually works."

"I need to finish some things up for the night. See you tomorrow."

I didn't wait for her to respond before I walked off. My feet and head felt heavy. The burn of pending tears crept up my throat, and I swallowed hard to keep it back as I entered my office.

How could I tell Hennie, or even Nolan for that matter, how terrified I was to have sex again? The last time I had, it was the most awful experience of my life. It had ended my marriage of six years, landed me in the hospital for hours, cost me thousands in legal fees and more in emotional turmoil as I went through the courts, not to mention the last two years of struggling to recover from such a deep trauma.

Claiming I wasn't ready felt like an understatement. I didn't know if I'd ever be ready. I would have to trust someone so deeply to open myself up like that. And yeah, I did hope that one day, that could be Nolan and me. But that day hadn't come, and I wasn't going to force it for the sake of stress relief. Even if my libido had been more demanding lately.

Nolan seemed content with our speed. We hadn't gotten around to really discussing the topic, but he knew I had hang ups in that department. He hadn't pressured me at all. As long as everyone involved was happy with the arrangement, I saw no reason to change things.

I realized that I had been staring at my laptop screen for the better part of an hour without comprehending what I was doing. Time to close things up for the night.

I shut down my laptop and stood to stretch. I needed to find my dog, eat a nice, hot meal, and get to bed early. Hopefully tomorrow would be better.

CHAPTER 16

I had woken up feeling unexpectedly lighter, and the sunny day helped to cheer me. At work, I'd been more productive that morning than I had in the several days before. Our new software was on its way. I just had to sit down and read up on how to install it and start testing it. I'd learn it and get it set up, then we could implement it after the Fourth of July rush.

When Sally came in for her shift, her mouth was stretched in the widest smile I'd ever seen. "Look what I got last night!"

The triangular Bishop purse hung from her shoulder on a leather strap. She turned from side to side to show it off.

"Wow," was all I could manage. I'd hoped it would look better in person, but sadly, it looked even more like a slice of pizza. Was there some kind of food-related fashion trend I'd missed? I almost asked, but didn't want to take the chance that she was unaware her accessory looked like dinner.

Sally gently placed her purse under the counter, then stood back to admire it.

"You can keep it in my office if that would be safer."

Sally looked at my office door, then back to her purse. "Umm... I think I'd rather have it in sight. But thank you. If I have to leave the counter, I'll put it in there."

"Sure." My phone rang, and I smiled when I saw Enid's name on the display. "Hey there."

"Oh, Thea, I didn't know when you'd be able to stop back over, and I couldn't leave today, but I just had to tell you."

"What's that?" I grabbed my notebook and returned to my office.

"Well, you remember that Marlene Kirby?"

"Of course." Just a little over a month ago, her twin sister had been pushed off the cliff at Ribbit Rock Overlook on our north hiking trail. I'd interviewed Marlene many times.

Enid continued. "Well, she's pregnant, you know, and she was just in the store with some girl friends. She told them that Mandy Rodgers isn't even pregnant. Faked the whole thing. Even showed up at the OB to make it seem real, pretending to have morning sickness." Enid made a *tsk*ing noise. "Sad, if you ask me, when a woman has to fake something like that to keep a man."

"Huh. Mandy told me that the only reason Jerry was going to leave his wife was because she was pregnant."

"There you have it, then."

"But what does that mean for the murder?"

"Oh, honey," Enid said, and I could picture her waving me off. "That's your department. I just bring the gossip. You figure out how to use it."

I chuckled. "Thanks, Enid. I will."

"And you'll tell me what comes of it?"

"Absolutely."

I ended the call and made a note. The lie made Mandy look more desperate, and if Barbara had been the one killed, Mandy would be the prime suspect. But why would she kill a man who she wanted badly enough to fake a pregnancy? If he'd turned her down, it would make sense. But he'd come to Cedar Fish with her after telling his wife he was leaving her.

Only one motive seemed possible. Money. With Jerry's handbag fame and wealth, if she had his child, she'd be entitled to part of his estate. But there would be no money until there actually was a child, and since the entire thing was a farce, killing him for money didn't fit too well, either. Besides, Mandy would have more fame and money if he lived, married her, and kept designing his purses.

Yet, she had kept the lie going. When I talked to her, she told me how Jerry's family would react to the news. And she'd made a comment about getting famous from a TV show of the murder. Maybe that was my explanation. She'd be able to cause drama and get attention with a pregnancy. And perhaps even more so if she claimed a loss when it was evident she wasn't pregnant.

I left my office and went outside to take Gar for a walk. The day continued to improve when I saw that the turtle had moved off the road. She was closer to the nest again. I didn't get it. In all the Googling I'd done, I found nothing to indicate that a turtle ever returned to its nest. Why was our turtle different?

Before Gar and I walked off, I saw where something had been digging to get under the wire fence surrounding the eggs. I assumed the kittens had been at it, but then I spotted a pile of raccoon leavings nearby. Nothing had gotten inside the enclosure from what I could tell, but I didn't want to trust that something wouldn't.

"Hey, keep an eye on the nest," I walkied to Nolan. "The kittens or Ricky are trying to dig their way in."

"Great." He sighed. "I'll see what I can do."

"I'm going to talk to Mandy again. Enid told me she lied about being pregnant, and I want to know why."

"Okay. But is there any point?"

"Maybe," I said. "I have an idea, but I want to talk to her to see if anything comes of it."

"Where's the Gar?"

"I'll drop him off."

I loaded Gar into my truck and drove until I found Nolan in the camper loop, working on one of the water hookups. I pulled up and Nolan whistled. Gar hopped out of the back, I waved to them both, then headed to Mandy's.

I planned what I would say as I drove. When I knocked on her door, I felt much less sympathy for her. If she'd lied, there was a reason. And maybe it was a deadly one.

Mandy opened the door, looking grey and tired. "Hi."

The tea gave me the perfect opening to get right to the point of why I was there. "Hey. Have the police talked to you about the tea?"

Mandy nodded. "They might arrest Barbara for it."

"I should hope so. That's attempted murder."

Mandy sucked in a breath and looked down.

"How are you feeling?" I asked.

"Tired. Sick."

"Do you have a virus or something? Since it can't be morning sickness."

Mandy looked up at me, confused. "What do you mean?"

"You're not pregnant, so it's not morning sickness."

Her mouth popped open. "I—" Her lower lip trembled and tears ran down her face. "How did you know?"

"I hear a lot of things. So, it's true? There is no baby?"

She shook her head and wiped her eyes. "I thought there was. I was late, you know, so I told him I was to see how he'd react. And it was so much better than I expected. How could I not keep lying when he said he'd leave his wife for me?"

Mandy broke into full-out sobs, and I glanced around to make sure no neighbors were watching. Luckily, her street was quiet and empty.

"Did you tell Jerry the truth?"

She shook her head. "He might've changed his mind."

"He might've." I narrowed my eyes slightly. "Or maybe he did find out and changed his mind, and that's why you killed him."

"What? No!" Mandy looked up at me with puffy, red eyes and an indignant expression. "I didn't do it! Even if he did somehow find out, he never told me. He loved me, and once he told Barbara it was over, that was it. He would have left her! He would have!"

Her hands balled into fists, and her whole face reddened. "It's not that hard to get pregnant, you know. I could have just gone and done it, and then it wouldn't have been a lie. Don't you think I would have tried that first before I killed the man I loved? Don't you think I would have done anything to have him?"

My initial urge was to point out that it was not, in fact, easy for everyone to get pregnant. In the better days with Russell, we'd tried, unsuccessfully, for years.

We'd talked about going the IVF route, but things had turned in our marriage, and I'd put it off. The years had gone by, and our marriage continued to deteriorate. I still felt the ache of not having children, but at the same time, immense relief that I was not tied indefinitely to my ex. I could live my life without ever having to see him again.

As I watched Mandy cry and shake, I thought she was sincere about her intentions. She would have done anything to have Jerry. Or she might have done anything to have his fame.

"Did you do it for money?" I blurted.

Her mouth popped open as tears continued to run down her face. "What?"

"Did you lie about being pregnant to get money from Jerry's estate?"

"I..." She shook her head and stared at me.

"Maybe you wanted his fame," I said, "so you killed him to be the famous murderer of the famous purse designer."

Her whole body quivered as she said, "I didn't kill him! I loved him!"

The more angry she became, the more I knew it was time to get out of there. She'd given me the answers I needed.

I held my hands up and took a step back. "Okay. You didn't." One more question came to mind. "Do you know anyone with diabetes?"

She blinked at me. "No. Why?"

I shrugged. "Just wondering. It's nothing. I'll let you go."

She glared as I backed off her front step and turned toward my truck. I got in and drove off, feeling guilty about how I'd gone about things. I didn't have to make her upset like that. Maybe Hennie and Nolan were right. The stress was getting to me, and I was getting sloppy. I cared less about being subtle and gently extracting information and more about getting someone to crumble and confess. It was like I'd gone from good cop to bad cop.

I had a strange feeling about Mandy. I had no idea how I'd know for sure, but I thought that Mandy's lie had been found out. Maybe she figured out a way she could get money, even if she didn't have a baby. And if he'd found out she was lying, then she easily could have killed him in anger for changing his mind and deciding not to leave Barbara after all.

I sat on these ideas as I returned to the campground. My phone buzzed with a text from Nolan before I arrived.

"You back yet?"

I called him rather than try to text while driving.

"I'm almost there," I said.

"Okay. Come to the beach when you get here."

"Why?"

"There's something you should see."

"I love it when you're cryptic," I said. "I'm pulling in now."

We hung up, and I continued down the main road, parking as close as I could to the beach. Nolan threw a stick and Gar ran after it, sending sand clumps into the air with each step.

"Hey there," I called to them.

When Gar snatched the stick in his mouth, he bounced over to bring it to me. I took it from him, rubbed his head, and threw the stick again. He took off with a yip and a hop.

As I neared Nolan, dread built in my stomach. Something sat on the sandy ground in front of him. Something big and dark and not moving. A fishy smell with a hint of rot hung in the air.

"What is that?" I asked.

"Dead alligator snapping turtle."

I stood beside him and looked at the spiky shell. It was bigger and darker than our other turtle's shell.

"I think it's a male," Nolan said.

"What killed it?"

"Not sure. Nothing obvious."

"Do you think it's the mate of our female turtle?"

He shrugged. "Probably. They're in the same area. There's not that many of them around." He stroked his beard and stared off. "I wonder..."

I raised an eyebrow and waited.

After another few moments, he said, "She keeps going back and forth to a water source, right?"

I nodded.

"What if we build another pond to keep her from crossing the road? We could put a little one near your cabin. I thought you might like that anyhow. Maybe add a nice, big, flat rock for the turtle to sun on so she's not tempted to sit in the entry."

"I wouldn't mind a pond," I said. "Maybe some koi?"

"The turtle would probably eat them, but sure."

"Oh. Forget that part. A pond would be nice. And if it kept the turtle off the road, I'd build two."

"I'll find a good spot and stake it out."

"That's a great idea." I tilted my head to the side, thinking. "I wonder if this is why she's being weird."

"What do you mean?"

"Female turtles don't come back to their nests after laying eggs. I've looked it up and Hennie confirmed it. I wasn't sure why she was doing some kind of bizarre, ultra-maternal, anti-turtle behavior, but this might explain it. Maybe she's looking for her mate. Or maybe she's afraid because she knows he's gone, and those eggs are all she has left of him."

Nolan raised an eyebrow at me. "Have you been reading romance novels?"

I stuck my tongue out. "Don't some animals mate for life? I think this is something that happens. The mate dies and the other one gets sad."

"We have a depressed turtle?"

"We might."

"Well, we better call the MDC about the dead turtle before we make the other one a therapy appointment."

"I'm on it. Reporting deaths is one of my specialities."

I drove back to the office and walked past Sally ringing up a camper at the front counter. I sat at my desk and brought up the number for the MDC. Jeanie Robinson took my call again.

"Hi, it's Thea Pagoni from Cedar Fish Campground," I said when she picked up.

"How's that turtle of yours doing?"

"She's weird, actually, but I think I know why. We found a dead turtle on the shore of our lake. We think it's her mate."

"I see," Jeanie said. "Well, that is one sad situation. I'll have someone come out to collect the body and investigate. Was there any obvious cause of death?"

"Not that we could see."

"Had anything changed in the environment, like new construction?"

"No, the lake is in the back of the campground, and it's pretty quiet there."

"Could someone have dumped something in the water?" she asked.

"I suppose it's possible. We have hundreds of people here every month. But we haven't found any evidence of that."

"I see." I heard a pen scratching and then, "Does the other turtle seem affected in any way?"

"Maybe? I read that turtles don't return to their nests, but this one keeps going back to her eggs."

"That is unusual." More scratching on paper. "I'll get someone out there today to investigate the death and check on the female."

"Thanks. I think people are interested in the nest. They gather around any time she's sitting out. And if there's any way that I can do something for the turtle, to get her to stop sitting on the road? I'm afraid she'll get hurt eventually."

"The agent can answer all of your questions when he's had the chance to inspect the situation."

"Thank you."

I hung up and thought about the turtle for a few minutes, until I was interrupted by Sally knocking on my door.

"Kimberly's here."

"Okay, thanks." I followed her out to the front counter.

I hadn't been expecting Kimberly. After our last encounter, I wasn't sure what this could be about. But she waited with her usual bright grin, and I relaxed.

"How are you doing?" I asked.

"Fabulous!" She waved a piece of paper in the air before smoothing it on the counter. "I had to come and show you this."

I glanced down at what looked to be some kind of official report.

"It's from the police," Kimberly continued. "My bakery has been thoroughly searched and tested, I was questioned *again*, and they said that no poisons or toxins of any kind were found. I'm no longer a suspect."

I nodded and glanced over the report. "Good. Glad to hear it since we have hundreds of cupcakes coming from your shop in a few days."

Her ponytail bounced as she nodded. "So, you can stop trying to make me look guilty now. Okay?"

"Sorry about that." I hadn't forgotten how quickly that sweet smile could turn sour. "This hasn't put you behind at all?"

"Kimmy Cakes would never miss a delivery."

"Good. While you're here, I might as well give you the final payment." I walked back into my office, peeled a check from the ledger, and filled it out. I took it back to the counter and handed it to Kimberly.

"Great!" She took a narrow notepad from her pocket and wrote out a receipt. "So glad you decided to go with Kimmy Cakes. Those cupcakes are going to be amazing!"

The door opened and Nolan walked in. He saw Kimberly, stopped, glanced around, narrowed his eyes, and walked back out.

I held in my laughter. I could only guess what he'd been looking for.

"I'm off." Kimberly collected her police report. "See you in a few days!"

She practically skipped out the door. I walked outside, too, to find Nolan. He swung slowly on the porch swing.

"What was that about?" I asked.

He flicked his gaze up at me. "Nothing."

"You were looking for cupcakes, weren't you?"

He met my eyes again and tried to look innocent. "I wanted to make sure you didn't need any help if she was delivering."

"Not until the fourth. Sorry," I said. "Someone's coming from the MDC."

"Good. Can I ask you something?" He shifted forward on the seat and put his fingertips together.

"Sure?" My heart sped at the way he hesitated.

"Can we have a proper date? Like go out to eat somewhere?"

Not half as bad as I had thought. I relaxed. "That would be nice."

He sat back. "Tonight?"

A smile broke across my face. "Can't wait." My heart leapt and fell into nervousness, which didn't really make sense. Nolan and I cooked for each other all the time. We'd spent plenty of date-like evenings together, walking around or hitting mini-golf balls. This felt different, though, and suddenly I was a nervous single woman going on a first date with an incredibly attractive man who I liked very much.

"So, why was Kimberly here?" he asked.

"The cops cleared her and her bakery. She wanted to tell me."

"And Mandy?"

"I don't know," I said. "I think she could have done something. She might be trying to get part of his estate. And the police might arrest Barbara for the tea."

"Might?"

"That's what I said. It's attempted murder. I don't know what they're waiting for."

"You better talk to her before they arrest her."

"Barbara?" I asked. "You're telling me to go talk to her?"

"Hadn't you planned to?"

"I got distracted with this turtle business. But yeah, I guess I should. Want to come along?"

"I want to be here for the MDC. I got the new pond staked out and need to make sure it'll be big enough." He got to his feet. "And I think Barbara will respond better to you alone."

I gave him a coy smile. "Since when do you trust me to talk to a potential murder suspect on my own?"

"I don't think she's dangerous like some of the others. Well, not dangerous to you."

"Then, I guess I'm off to go interrogate the suspect."

"Be careful, though." He pulled me close and kissed me.

"I will."

I watched him walk off and sighed. Some part of me wanted things to get physical with him. And not a small part.

CHAPTER 17

I drove to Barbara's feeling more nervous than I usually did when going to question someone. Maybe it was because she'd already gotten somewhat aggressive with me. I should have told Nolan the truth—that I wanted him to come with me because Barbara kind of scared me.

I pulled up to her house and took a deep breath, then approached her door. Before she answered, I changed my planned tactic entirely. It would take some acting and lying, but would likely have a much better outcome than if I started accusing her of trying to poison Mandy.

Barbara yanked the door open and puckered her lips. "You."

"Hey, Barbara. I wondered if I might talk to you for a minute?"

"About?"

I made a point of looking around before I leaned closer and whispered conspiratorially. "I... wanted to get your help with something."

She raised an eyebrow and stepped aside to let me in. Her house was much nicer than Mandy's: expensive lamps and vases, professional-quality styling, tidier and better kept. Barbara gestured to indicate her sitting room. I sat on one of the overstuffed chairs and rested my elbows on my knees, letting my nervousness show.

"I would appreciate if you didn't tell anyone that I came here to talk to you," I said.

Barbara sat in the chair beside me. "Can't promise until I hear why you're here."

I blew out a breath. "Like I said, I need your help." I shifted and looked at my hands before meeting her gaze. "I know about the tea you gave Mandy. Water hemlock was in the book you took out recently from the library, and you have it growing in your backyard, so I know that you know how deadly it is. And I know that's why you put it in the tea you gave Mandy."

Barbara narrowed her eyes and pushed her lips out, but said nothing.

"That's what I need your help with. There's someone I want to... give some friendship tea to. I was hoping you could tell me how to go about it?"

Barbara stared at me for a long time. She glared and looked me over, then sat back. "Who are you trying to poison?"

I gulped and thought of the most honest answer I could give. "My ex." I chuckled nervously and rolled my eyes. "You know how men are."

Barbara harrumphed. "You're better off without him."

I nodded. "But it would make my life easier if I were *really* without him, you know what I mean?"

Barbara narrowed her eyes at me again. "I doubt I can help you. I got lucky with the water hemlock. It grew here, and I thought it was Queen Anne's lace. I had picked it and used it in a floral arrangement for my sitting room until someone told me what it really was. And what can I say? I read a lot of mysteries."

"That's where you got the idea?"

"It was the murder weapon in a book I read. Since I had the plant already, it made sense. I thought it'd be easy enough to play dumb. Claim that I thought it was Queen Anne's lace and get myself off the hook. It was a good plan."

I almost asked if the police had questioned her yet, but realized that would reveal that I'd had something to do with her imminent arrest. Did Barbara have any idea that she might be going away for years?

"Weren't you worried about getting caught?" I asked.

She lifted a shoulder. "Like I said, I read a lot of mysteries. I know something about not getting caught. If someone did die, no one would ever find out I did it."

I was shocked at her arrogance. And her stupidity. How many criminals thought the same thing before they landed themselves in jail?

I shrugged. "I guess it worked with Jerry."

She shook her head. "No. That wasn't me. Don't get me wrong, I've thought about it plenty over the years. Planned it out a few times. I would have made him suffer more, though. I might've gone through with it. I don't know. Would have depended on how much I got in the divorce. He might've been worth more to me alive if it meant sizable support payments."

"Oh." I acted surprised. "I thought you had done it. It was an impressive murder. Seemed like something you could pull off."

"Oh, I could. I'm regretting that I didn't. But that makes it easier for me. I have nothing to hide."

"I don't blame you for wanting to kill him. If my husband cheated on me like that, I would, too."

"I got used to the cheating part," she said. "The thing is, when men cheat, they make up for it in other ways." She gestured around the room. "I buy whatever I want. Plus, I never had to have sex with him. It was like having a wealthy roommate. Decent setup, really."

"But if he'd left, you would have lost all that. Makes sense why you tried to stop it."

"Exactly. I mean, believe me, I'm not lacking physical affection. I've got my own boy on the side. And why shouldn't I when Jerry had so many flings?"

"Good for you. Why should you suffer when he's the one causing all the problems?"

"You get it." She nodded. "The timing couldn't have been any better. Not only do I not have to put up with Jerry and all his little hussies, I get his life insurance and social security benefits on top of the entire Bishop Purses estate. And Mandy gets nothing! He didn't update his will!" Barbara laughed once. "I wish whoever killed him had done it a lot sooner."

I forced a chuckle. "Wow. That does sound good. I wish I would have been so lucky with my ex. It would've saved me a ton of money and hassle if someone else had taken him out." After I said it, guilt stabbed my chest. It felt a little close to the truth to pretend I was planning to poison Russell. He had taken everything from me and more. I hated him deeply, but I was never the type to wish him dead.

"Sounds like you have a plan to fix him," Barbara said.

"Right." I nodded. "Thanks for chatting. You've given me some ideas."

She gave me a thin, knowing smile. "Hope it works out for you."

We stood and I followed her back to the front door.

"Take care," I said as I walked back to my truck.

I drove off, tapping the steering wheel while chewing on my lower lip and feeling unsettled. Thinking of Russell had stirred my emotions. The anger, the bitterness, the outrage. I breathed in slowly, trying to reclaim some calmness. I distracted myself by thinking of my date with Nolan, just a few hours away. What in the world was I going to wear?

I'd tried on two different outfits and considered a third. Gar watched me from the corner of my bedroom as I tossed another skirt onto the bed. Nolan had never seen me dressed up. I wanted to get the first time right.

I settled on a simple black sundress. Little black dresses had never let me down before. I picked a pair of earrings and a necklace to accessorize, but I didn't want to go too far. This was still Outer Branson. The restaurants wouldn't exactly be black tie.

I finished my makeup and slipped into the most unpractical pair of shoes I owned—my shiny, red heels. I knew I wouldn't get to wear them often, but I hadn't been able to part with them during my clothing purge when I'd sold my house.

Nolan knocked on my door, and I picked up my purse.

"Behave yourself tonight," I told Gar.

I opened the door and Nolan's eyes grew round when he saw me. "Whoa."

I felt a rush of warmth and took a moment to admire him back. He wore a burgundy collarless shirt over casual khaki pants. The shirt was just fitted enough to show off his chest and arms.

"You clean up nice yourself," I said.

He held out his arm, and I took it as we walked to his truck. He opened my door to help me in.

When he slid into the driver's seat, he turned to me. "There's a decent Italian place in town. Want to give it a try?"

"Sure."

He drove out of the campground, and silence fell between us for a few minutes. We usually talked all day to each other, so why did we suddenly have nothing to say?

After a while, Nolan said, "I got that leaky washing machine under control today."

"Oh. I didn't even know we had a leaky washing machine."

"Those machines are getting pretty old."

I sighed. "Yeah. Along with everything else."

"I think we can squeeze a few more years out of them."

I nodded, but I didn't want to think or talk about the campground for one night. There was still so much I didn't know about Nolan. A thousand different questions ran through my mind, but I settled for, "Have you talked to your family lately?"

"I have. They're actually coming up for a few days over the Fourth."

"Oh, really?" I gulped. I hadn't been prepared for an answer like that. "That'll be nice. They've never been to the campground before, have they?"

"No. They're not huge campers, but they wanted to see what I've been up to. My parents are coming and one of my brothers with his family."

"That sounds nice." It sounded completely over-whelming. All my plans for the event somehow felt cheap and lame when I thought about his family seeing it all and judging me by it.

We pulled up to the restaurant and walked inside. As I expected, not nearly the high-end establishment I'd been to occasionally back in St. Louis, but for a small town, it was tastefully decorated and romantically lit.

We were seated and I looked over the menu. I read description after description, but nothing made my mouth water.

"What are you getting?" I asked.

"The mega trio."

The menu listed the trio as a piece of lasagna, chicken parmesan, and fettuccine Alfredo. "That's a lot of food."

He grinned. "I know. What about you?"

"Not sure." I could always pick a simple chicken and pasta, but none of the sauces seemed appetizing.

The waiter came over, and I had to tell him I still wasn't ready.

I read over the menu again and tried to narrow it down. "Maybe I'll just get the fish."

Nolan nodded and raised his hand to call attention to the waiter.

"Wait." I looked back at my other non-pasta choices. "Never mind. I guess that'll work."

"You sure?"

I nodded. "Yeah. You order first though."

The waiter returned and Nolan gave his order. I hesitated one more time, then decided the fish was my safest option.

When the waiter left, I covered my face. "I'm not the biggest fan of Italian. Sorry. I should have said something earlier."

"Do you want to go somewhere else?"

"No, no. I'm not anti-Italian, it's just not my favorite. Guess that makes me a traitor."

"How so?"

"Shouldn't someone with an Italian last name like Italian food?"

He shrugged. "Are you sure Pagoni is Italian?"

"Aren't all names that end in a vowel?"

"I don't think so. What about Moore or White?"

"Those are Es. That doesn't count."

He raised an eyebrow. "Garcia? Isn't that Spanish?"

"Oh. You're right." I pulled my eyebrows together. "My mom always said last names that end in vowels are

Italian. I guess I never questioned some things my parents told me."

He chuckled. "I know what you mean. My dad always drinks water with every cup of coffee because he says coffee dehydrates you. I believed him and did the same for years. But it doesn't."

I gave him a crooked smile. "Maybe our parents don't know everything after all."

Our food came, and I was pleasantly surprised by the fish I'd ordered. It tasted buttery with lemon and herbs—more flavorful than I expected. Nolan's meal looked more like three meals. I couldn't see how he'd fit so much food inside his stomach.

"How'd it go with the MDC?" I asked as I dug into my fish. So much for not talking about the campground.

Nolan swallowed a bite. "Fine. He took the body, but didn't have any helpful ideas."

"Oh."

"What about Barbara? How'd that go?" He finished off his piece of lasagna and moved onto his chicken.

I shrugged. "I pretended I needed her help poisoning someone to see if she would confess. She admits she wanted to kill Jerry and that she's glad he's gone, but still claims it wasn't her."

"Geez." He shook his head and swallowed the last bite of chicken. "My dad and brother will probably ask about the investigation."

"Will they help us solve it?"

"They might have ideas, but they can't really get involved."

"The thing is," I said, "Barbara probably did it, but I can't prove it. She even said that if she ever committed murder, no one would know. That's why she wouldn't admit it to me. She's smart enough not to fall for that. And I think, after talking to Kimberly, that she's involved. It would make the perfect crime if they worked together."

A forkful of fettuccine went into Nolan's mouth. He chewed, swallowed, and said, "They'll have to arrest Barbara soon for the tea. Then they can determine if she had anything to do with Jerry's death."

"I guess the police will have to figure this one out," I said. "I'm at a loss for evidence. It's going nowhere."

"My dad and brother might have some suggestions."

"I hope so."

"You gonna finish that?" He'd eaten the last of his meal and eyed the few bites of fish I'd left.

I pushed my plate toward him. "All yours."

Nolan cleared the plate and sat back to rub his stomach. "I'm stuffed."

"That was a lot of food."

"Yeah. It was good." He glanced at the menu card sitting at the end of the table. "You want dessert?"

"You're not serious."

"Always room for pie."

I laughed. "I'm good."

He decided against the pie and ordered the check instead when the waiter asked. We got up to leave, and another couple stood up from their stools at the bar.

I grabbed Nolan's arm and hid behind him. "It's Mark and Linda Dorsey."

Mark stumbled forward but caught himself on the stool.

"And they're drunk," Nolan said.

CHAPTER 18

Mark glanced toward Nolan and squinted at him. Probably, Mark wouldn't recognize Nolan as easily as he would me.

Nolan turned his head toward me. "We'll just walk quickly, not make eye contact, and not say anything, okay?"

"Okay."

I kept my head down and clung to Nolan's arm as we walked by.

"Well, if it isn't my favorite customer," Mark said.

Nolan pushed the door open and held it for me. The door shut behind us but quickly opened again. My heart pounded in my ears as I clutched Nolan harder.

"Oh, that's right," Mark said loudly, following us through the lot. "I guess you're not a customer anymore, are you?"

I looked to Nolan and he shook his head.

"We should report you," Linda added.

"Yeah!" Mark said. "It's not right, what you did!"

Nolan turned sharply between two parked cars to cross the row and kept his arm securely around me. When Mark and Linda followed us, Nolan paused to address them. "Why don't you call a cab and get home safe?"

Mark stopped and crossed his arms, swaying just feet from Nolan. "What are you going to do if I don't?"

Nolan crossed his arms also. "Nothing, because you're going to keep walking."

Mark lunged at Nolan. Nolan simply stepped to the side, and Mark, in his drunken state, stumbled and fell to his hands and knees. Linda dashed to him and helped him up.

"Look what you've done now!" she shouted. "Wasn't ruining our vacation bad enough?!"

Linda's triangular Bishop purse was slung over her shoulder. She grabbed the handle and whipped the bag at Nolan. He held an arm up to block it. I put my fists up, expecting she would come for me next. I tried to guess what angle she would attack from and how I could fight back best.

"Thea." Nolan put his arm across my waist and slid me behind him as he stepped back.

Linda swung again. Her attack threw her off balance, and she tripped into Mark. They caught each other, but it was enough of a distraction that we'd backed several feet away by the time they recovered.

Nolan handed me his keys. "Get in the truck."

I turned and ran the last few feet to the truck. I slid into the passenger seat and leaned over to start the engine. Nolan hopped in a moment later. He shut the door, and Mark banged on the glass with his fists.

"This isn't over!" he shouted.

Nolan pressed on the gas slowly. If it'd been me, I would have stomped on it, but I guess he was more concerned with not hitting Mark than I would have been.

I twisted in the seat to watch as Nolan hurried out of the parking lot. Mark and Linda stood shaking their fists at us.

My blood soared through my veins, and my hands shook as I buckled my seatbelt.

"You okay?" Nolan asked.

"I think so? Are you?"

He nodded and looked in his rearview mirror.

"I can't believe how far they're going over a few thousand dollars," I said. "Makes me extra glad we didn't hire them. If he can be like this over a cancelled contract, who knows what he might do if things went wrong during an event."

Nolan checked his mirrors again. "They're both not right."

I shivered and wrapped my arms around my middle. "I'm afraid they're going to come after me."

Nolan reached over to squeeze my hand. "Not gonna lie. I've been concerned. I looked into the two of them a bit. Mark has a record. And now Linda does, too."

"How can she be out and getting drunk so soon after being arrested for burglary?"

"It's her first offense, the property damage was minimal, and the amount stolen didn't come to much. She must've posted bail."

"Should we call the cops about what just happened?"

"I would call about them driving drunk, but OBPD will never get there in time." Nolan pulled his mouth to the side. "Besides that, there's not much the police can do since there was no actual assault. But, it'll likely piss Mark and Linda off pretty bad. It could cause problems for Linda, if she's out on bail. Might be better to let it go than to push them."

"So, it would have been better if they'd actually attacked us."

"I wouldn't say better, but they would have gotten themselves arrested and charged."

"I don't want to just sit around, waiting for them to do something else." I shivered and wrapped my arms tighter.

"Hopefully they won't. You sleep with your gun near your bed, right?"

I nodded. "What if...?"

He looked over questioningly.

"I don't know. Is it a coincidence that Linda was in the store just before Jerry on the day he died?"

Nolan narrowed his eyes in thought.

I gasped. "There was a test strip. In the things recovered from Linda's possession after the robbery. Either she or Mark must have diabetes. Which means easy access to insulin."

Nolan's jaw tightened, and he said nothing for several minutes.

A thought crept into my mind that was so terrifying, I pushed it back until it wouldn't be silenced. "What if she meant to kill me? What if I was the target, but she missed and got Jerry instead? I just don't know how she went about it."

Nolan slid his gaze to me and then back. "Didn't Jerry take your muffin that had been sitting on the counter?"

"Yeah, but that was before Linda was there. Could she have put the insulin in something else and given it to him? Or snuck up behind him and stuck him with a needle?"

"Why would she do that if you were the target? You said there's no connection between Linda and Jerry."

"True." Every time I had an idea, it quickly fell apart. "Maybe she wasn't trying to kill me, but is working with Barbara for money. She robbed two places to get a few hundred bucks. Why wouldn't she kill for money, too?"

"I don't think hiring hitmen is as common as you think."

I shrugged. "Something has to add up. It wasn't an accident. So, who killed Jerry and how? Could the insulin be a distraction for something else?"

"Like?"

"Like... it's hiding some other sort of poison?"

"That's not how it works."

I growled under my breath. "It has to all go together somehow!"

He patted my knee. "We'll figure it out."

"I'm not so sure this time." I considered again. "Maybe Linda was the distraction and Mark snuck into the campground and did it."

"There's still no motive that we know of for Mark and Linda to kill Jerry. But, you can review the tapes again and see if he shows up anywhere."

"Good idea. We can look at them when we get back."

"When we get back?" He raised an eyebrow. "Is our date over then?"

"Did you have something else in mind?"

He lifted a shoulder as he turned into the campground. "We could walk a little while. Or just sit and talk."

"I could use a walk. But I'll need different shoes."

He parked at my cabin, and we both hopped out of his truck. After crossing to my side, he took my hand, then pulled me close. His hand slid to my cheek and his other arm wrapped around my waist. He kissed me longer and harder than usual. When he pulled back, he whispered into my ear, "Or we could just hang out a little while."

I swallowed hard and wiggled away to give myself room. "Maybe not tonight."

He kissed my hand and smiled. "How about we walk the east trail? Have you ever been to Echo Cave at night?"

"No. That sounds great. Let me just go change."

I dashed inside my cabin and grabbed my sneakers. For a moment, I considered taking Gar along, but puppies and bats didn't always mix well, and I didn't want to have to cut our time short if Gar decided to bark at the bats. I laced up my sneakers, gave Gar a thorough petting, and went back outside to where Nolan was waiting.

He took a few steps in the direction of the east trail, and I let him lead me. We cut across Hook Loop and passed a few campers walking along with flashlights. Others sat at campfires, roasting hotdogs or marshmallows.

This time of night, the trail was technically closed, though nothing would stop someone from going down it. No artificial lighting lined our path, and the trees on either side of us were thick overhead. The round moon sent intermittent rays through the leaves to guide our way. The crickets sang in full chorus, and when I could see the sky through the trees, the stars sparkled on an indigo backdrop.

The heat coming from Nolan's hand in mine radiated up my arm and warmed my core.

"I don't want to rush you," he said after a long silence. "I know it might be difficult for you after what happened with your ex. But I'd like to have an idea of where I stand, physically."

I nodded and felt my throat grow thick. "That's fair. So don't hate me for saying I don't know."

After a pause, he said, "I'm not sure what to do with that."

"All I know for sure is that I'm not ready yet."

He nodded slowly. "That's what I needed to know."

"Sorry."

"Don't be. You've been through a lot."

"Yeah." I let silence fall for a few moments, then added, "Just know that it's not a lack of wanting. I *want* to, I'm just... afraid."

He gave me a mischievous half smile. "So long as it's not a lack of wanting."

"Definitely not."

He squeezed my hand tighter and a shiver of thrill ran across my skin. Good thing he didn't know just how much wanting there really was.

We walked for another few minutes, and then he paused. "Listen." He pointed to a black swoosh in the sky. "We're close. They're everywhere."

When I listened past the thumping of my heart, I could hear the squeaking of the bats. It was difficult to see them, but when there was a clear patch of sky, several black smears crossed the space.

The cave sat a few feet off the trail. A sign marked it as Echo Cave and warned visitors not to disturb the bats. During the day, people could stand in the cave and look up and see hundreds of bats sleeping overhead. At night, the cave was almost empty.

"Why does it feel creepier without the bats?" I asked softly.

"Your spidey sense knows that something lives here."

I gazed up at the dark ceiling of the cave. Light didn't reach too far in, so we stopped a few feet from the entrance and stood beside the wall of darkness.

"I feel like something could jump out of the black and get me." I stepped out of the cave and back into the moonlit night.

Fear mixed into my tumble of emotions. Nolan stepped out to join me. I shivered, and he wrapped me in a hug.

"I'll save you from the bats," he said.

"Thanks." I rested my head on his shoulder.

"Nice night," he said.

"Yeah." Nice as it was, I still felt creeped out. "Can we head back?"

We started down the trail, and he took my hand again.

"You don't talk about your parents and sister much," he said.

"I don't talk to them much, I guess. I sent them both texts to see if they could come for the holiday. My mom said she thought they were busy, and my sister never got back to me."

"That sucks."

"We all lived pretty busy lives in the city. Well, they still do. My sister has kids, my parents both work. I'm the odd one out."

"When was the last time you saw them?" he asked.

"Right before I came to the campground. I had dinner with them all."

We had wound our way back to my cabin. Nothing more was said as Nolan walked me to the door.

He gave me a long kiss, then stepped back. "Thanks for a great night."

"You, too. And thanks for dinner. The food was better than I expected."

"Must be that Italian finally coming out."

"Maybe."

I stood on my porch for a moment, watching him walk to his truck. He got in and lifted a hand to wave goodbye before driving off.

I opened my front door and was attacked by Gar. He jumped all over me and licked my face.

"Hello, hello," I said. "I missed you, too."

I let him outside to do his business and run around to burn off energy. As I watched him sniff and bounce through the yard, my thoughts drifted to Nolan.

It had been a great night. Mostly. Nolan and I had gotten a little deeper into our lives, though the enjoyable parts of the night were interwoven with the scarier encounter with Mark and Linda. Sad to think our first real date almost ended in a fistfight.

After I let Gar back inside, I got into bed but lay awake for some time. My mind wouldn't settle, and the weight in my chest made my breath feel tight. As I strained to hear every sound around me, I realized how afraid I really felt. I checked twice that my gun was loaded and within easy reach before I fell asleep.

Chapter 19

In the morning, I made strong coffee and downed half my mug before sitting in my office to review the camera footage from last night. If Mark or Linda had shown up, I wanted to know. I started with the camera at the outside corner of the store and worked my way through the campground.

Throughout the night, the most interesting thing I saw was a late-night fan kneeling at Jerry's memorial and crying for several minutes. I noticed that some of the photos and flowers that were against the fence had been chewed and torn. I shook my head. Had to be the goats. But no sign of Mark or Linda or anything else out of the ordinary.

I was about to move on, when something caught my attention near the wildlife area. A storage shed housed the food and other maintenance supplies and equip-

ment for the animals. At the back corner of the shed, I
saw fast-paced movement that looked like digging.

I zoomed in closer to see what was going on. I recognized the thick, striped tail and gasped. "Ricky!"

Gar, sleeping under the desk, jumped at my outburst.

"Sorry boy." I petted him and returned my attention
to the footage.

Ricky had dug a hole and found a way into the shed.
His little body wriggled out of sight and I waited. Minutes later, he reemerged with what looked to be very
full cheeks.

I shook my head. That raccoon had been nothing but
a headache since Hennie caught him and tried to give
him to me as a pet.

I grabbed my walkie talkie and called Nolan. "Take
a close look at the feed shed when you get a minute. I
just watched camera footage of Ricky breaking in and
making off with the goods."

"Man, he gets into everything."

"I can deal with a little stolen goat feed so long as he
leaves those turtle eggs alone."

"He has so far. I'll let you know what I find at the
shed."

I put down my walkie and decided to go back further
in my footage review. I found the moment Linda's car
appeared in our front lot on the day Jerry was killed.
No one was in the car with her. I checked other cameras

during that time and saw no sign of Mark. I didn't see his car anywhere, either.

I rested my head in my hands and stared at my computer screen. It seemed clear that Mark hadn't gotten to Jerry. But who had?

A knock on my door made me look up. "Hey Sally."

She glanced over her shoulder, then said quietly, "Someone is asking what the turtle's name is. I didn't know what to tell them."

"Oh. Uhh..." I looked around for ideas but couldn't think of a decent turtle's name on the spot. "Spike" seemed like a bit much. "Tell them that we're having a naming contest, and if they want to write down a suggestion, they can include their name and phone number and I'll call them if their name wins."

"How fun! Can anyone enter?" Sally's expression turned hopeful.

"Sure."

"Even employees?"

"Why not."

"Oh, and what do they win?"

"Uhh..." What could I afford to give away? "How about a free night of camping?"

"Neat!" Sally turned away, and I heard her excitedly telling the camper about the contest.

I closed my door. Before I forgot what I told her, I typed some simple details onto a small poster and printed it. I dug around under the front counter and found an old box from receipt tape. I punched a hole in the top for the entries and taped the details to the front of the box.

"There we go." I showed it to Sally and set it on the front counter. "Now we're official."

"I texted my husband to tell my boys," she said. "They're so excited and thinking up lots of names. Oh, is there a limit to how many names can be entered?"

"No. We can use plenty of suggestions."

"Goody!" She clapped her hands and sent another text.

I picked up the walkie talkie and told Nolan and Curtis, "We now have an official turtle-naming contest. They can enter in the office."

Nolan walked through the door a few minutes later.

"Got a name for the turtle?" I asked.

"Nope. Her pond is almost done, though." He leaned against the counter. "So, that hole in the shed?" Nolan shook his head and chuckled.

I narrowed my eyes. "How bad?"

"Ricky got more than a little goat feed. Almost an entire 50-pound bag is gone."

I clenched my jaw and reached for my cup of ice. "That raccoon is taking years off my life."

"I'll patch the hole in the shed and reinforce it before filling the outside hole back in. Hopefully that'll keep him out."

"I wonder if there's some kind of natural raccoon repellant." I still had that book of dangerous plants. Maybe it could tell me something.

"I don't know of any."

I sighed. "Thanks."

He smiled and dipped his head to me before leaving the office. I sighed with contentment and felt the warmth rise in my chest. The feeling was familiar, and when I recognized it, a flood of panic followed. I couldn't be falling for Nolan. I wasn't ready for that yet.

I took Gar outside for a walk to clear my head. When we made our way back toward the office, we spotted Hennie, on her way to find me.

"I need the updates!" she demanded after parking her four-wheeler.

I told her about my conversation with Barbara and my suspicions of Mark and Linda after the terrible encounter we had with them.

"Okay, but now the real details," Hennie said.

"That's everything. I did review the videos this morning and didn't see Mark."

"Not that! You and Nolan. Your hot date." She rubbed her hands together and licked her lips.

"Oh." I sighed. "It was nice. We went to dinner, then for a walk down to Echo Cave. I told him I wasn't ready to make things physical."

"What'd he say about that?" she asked.

"He's fine with it." I chewed my lip. "I assured him it wasn't a lack of desire."

"Then why don't you follow your heart, shut up your head, and go for it?"

"What if I freak out in the middle of it? I don't want to ruin things. I'm meeting his parents and brother soon. It all feels too real and serious all of a sudden."

Hennie put her hands on my shoulders. "You got a good man there. Stop worrying so much. See what happens."

"I don't want another disaster relationship like the last one."

"Don't blame ya. But if you don't take a risk, you can't get something good."

"It has been nice having someone again. Even if it's just casual. I like being in a relationship. And Nolan doesn't make me feel suffocated."

Hennie nodded and waited eagerly.

"That's all I'm going to say. That and we have a solution for the turtle."

"And what about this Mark and Linda? We gonna talk to them?"

"I don't know about that." The idea of facing either of them again made my chest tight with dread. "I think I'd rather let the police do the interrogating."

"That's not like you."

"If my theory is correct, that means I was the original murder target, not Jerry." Saying it out loud again sent a wave of terror shivering through me. "What if they decide to finish the job?"

Hennie's eyebrows pulled into a frown. "When you put it like that... If you ever feel afraid, you come to my place, now. I have plenty of guns, animals, and karate skills." She stepped back and kicked high in the air, then did a combination blocking-attack move.

"Thanks." I also knew Nolan would sleep on my couch if I asked him to. "I still don't think confronting Linda would get me anywhere with them."

"Let's think about this." She paced across the road. Gar watched and tried to get her to pet him every time she paused to turn. She stopped and faced me. "I got nothing. You're the sleuther."

"I need to go back to when Linda and Jerry were in the store. Maybe I missed something before."

Hennie followed me into my office, and I pulled up the footage on my computer. We scrolled through Kimberly and me talking at the counter. The police had cleared her, so I didn't want to waste more time looking at her as a suspect. I slowed down the footage at the end of our conversation.

"Okay, so that's where I ate the muffin and put it down." I pointed to the screen. The muffin was blocked from the camera by the register. "Keep your eyes on that spot."

Hennie nodded and moved closer to the screen, squinting as she concentrated.

I hit play again, and we watched Jerry come into the store for the first time. When he pointed to the muffin, I said, "Here's where he snatches it."

Jerry took out his wallet and handed me a dollar. As I put it in the register and took out four quarters, Jerry moved his hand near the muffin's location. The register blocked his action, but it looked like he shoved something into his pocket. He purchased a few items, then left the store.

"So, we can watch on the outside camera now and see him feed the goats." I switched the video feed, and we watched for a few minutes. When Jerry walked away, we switched back to the store-camera feed.

"Jerry comes back inside right after Linda leaves." I rewound the part of the video where they almost passed each other. They were never in close enough proximity, so there was no chance of her slipping him something or injecting him.

"Where's the part of Linda being in the store?" Hennie asked.

I brought up the clip of my first unpleasant conversation with Linda. As we watched, there was the moment when I'd gotten fed up and turned away from her. She had dug in her purse for something, but the bag itself hid whatever she was doing.

"Here's where Jerry comes back in." We watched as Jerry requested quarters for the feed machine. He scooped the quarters off the counter and then walked out.

"Wait a second." I backed the video up. "What's that?"

In Jerry's shorts pocket, a large bulge could be seen—and not the center bulge that I'd been told about.

"That looks like the muffin." I went back to when he first walked in. "No bulge!" I pointed excitedly and rewound the video to watch it again. "I assumed Jerry had taken the muffin the first time he came in, when he asked about it. But if he didn't take it until the second time, that was *after* Linda came in!"

In my excitement, I scrolled the video back to Linda. I watched extra closely where the muffin had been sitting. This time, when I saw her dig into her purse, it was obvious to me that she did something with her hands right where the muffin was.

I sat back in my chair and let the shock pass through me. "That was it. Right there. She does something to the muffin, thinking it was mine. Then Jerry steals it and eats it and that's it."

Hennie raised an eyebrow and watched the video one more time. "Hard to say, but I think you could be right. Can't see for sure, is the problem."

"But it's so obvious now that you see it, don't you think?"

"Seems so. What'd she do to the muffin though? We know it wasn't poisoned."

"If Jerry died of low blood sugar and insulin causes that, she must've put insulin in the muffin."

Hennie nodded and pulled her eyebrows together. "You might have it. But is it enough to convict her?"

"Better be."

Chapter 20

"See? See!" I pointed at the screen as Nolan watched the video.

"I see." He looked at me for a long moment. I wasn't sure I understood his expression. "You're telling me the only reason you're alive right now is because you weren't in the mood for a blueberry muffin that day?"

When he said it like that, my body went cold all over. "Good thing you didn't see it and eat my leftovers."

His eyebrows raised for a moment. He probably hadn't considered that, but if he'd seen the muffin and knew I didn't want it, he'd certainly have eaten it.

Hennie shook her head and held her hands up. "Don't go get yourselves all worked up. If you'd been hungry enough to eat the muffin, it would have been gone before Linda came in.

"Maybe," I said. "But she might've found something else." I glanced at my plastic travel mug of ice, sitting a few feet from me on the counter. I reached over to pick it up. "I'll be careful not to leave my food or drinks where someone could tamper with them."

Nolan didn't appear consoled by Hennie's reasoning, either. "Did you call the police?"

"No. I wanted to show you first and make sure I wasn't crazy."

He shook his head. "It's enough to get them a solid lead. I don't know that they'll be able to prove anything, and that worries me."

"I'll call them."

He stood and headed toward the door, but turned back. He walked over, wrapped his arms tight around me, and kissed the top of my head. "Please. Be careful."

I nodded, my throat still thick with fear. "You too."

He held my gaze for an intense moment. "I don't know what I'd do if something happened to you."

I was suddenly very aware of Hennie's presence—just feet from us—hearing every word and seeing every expression.

I stepped back from him and scratched my neck as I looked down. "I better call them."

He left the office. Before Hennie could say anything, I held up a finger. "Don't."

She chuckled and patted my shoulder. "This is highly entertaining, watching you two pretend you're not in love."

I picked up my phone and called the police. When I got Longshore on the line, I said, "I have some information on the murder of Jerry Bishop. I have reason to believe that Linda Dorsey poisoned him by accident when she tried to kill me."

Longshore paused for a moment, then whistled. "Someone tried to kill you?"

"Seems that way."

"I can't imagine any reason why."

Irritation flared in my chest at his hint of sarcasm. "It was a business deal gone wrong," I explained. "My video footage shows that Linda had access to the muffin that Jerry ate right before he died."

"Access to it? Access doesn't mean she did something to it."

"She did, though. She and her husband keep threatening me, and Linda had a blood-sugar test strip in her bag the night of the robbery. That's how Jerry died. It all makes sense."

"I'm sure it does to you, and we always *appreciate* your insight." The sarcasm wasn't quite as hidden this time.

If he wasn't going to suppress his true feelings, then neither was I. "This would make the third murder I solved, so I think it'd probably be a good idea if you sent that detective down to watch this video so he can go arrest the killer before I make a citizen's arrest. I don't think that would make you guys look too good."

Longshore cleared his throat. "We'll be there just as soon as time allows."

"Thank you," I said sweetly. "I look forward to it."

I slammed the phone down on my desk. "Why do they have to be so incompetent!"

Hennie shook her head. "Men don't like it when you show them up, honey. Get used to it."

"But this is murder. *My* possible murder. I need to start making phone calls. Get that Longshore and Randall out of there."

Hennie nodded. "I know you're mad, and I would be, too. But let's see if they can't catch her before you go getting them fired. Might need their help."

"If I relied on them, I'd already be dead. If it weren't for Nolan—" His name stuck in my throat as I thought of all the times he'd saved me. I closed my eyes and breathed deeply. "Maybe I need to carry my gun on me."

"Been saying that for weeks now."

"I know, I just didn't want to admit I was in that much danger."

"Never know when something will come at you."

I took my nervous energy outside to pace while waiting. When the police arrived almost an hour later, I was even more disappointed to see that it was officers Randall and Longshore and not Detective Hooley. What were my chances of getting anywhere with these two?

I gestured for them to follow me inside and whispered as I passed Hennie, "Tweedle Dee and Dum are here."

"Let me show you what I'm seeing on the video," I told the officers.

"We were under the impression that we had the security video in our possession already," Longshore said. "It's on the report."

"There's a backup system," I explained.

He exchanged a look with Officer Randall. Nolan had warned that it'd be better if they didn't know I always had access to the video footage, but I didn't see how I could lie at this point.

When they said nothing else, I played the footage and explained, "You can see where Linda tampers with the muffin and then Jerry takes it."

"You can't see what she's doing," Randall protested.

"But you know the muffin is there and you can see her doing *something*," I said.

"Get to the part where Jerry takes it," Longshore said.

I forwarded the video.

"There's nothing to see on that one, either," Longshore said.

"Look at the bulge in his pocket. He clearly has the muffin, and the wrapper was found on him later."

"The wrapper." Longshore flipped through a thin stack of papers he'd brought in a folder. "The goat ate it. We don't know for certain it was Jerry's at all."

"But the goat ate Jerry's shorts, and that's where the wrapper was."

"We don't have proof of that," Randall said.

"But—" I blinked at them and looked to Hennie for support.

"How's about that tea?" Hennie asked. "Did you ever look into Barbara?"

Her question didn't really help me now, but I did want to know the answer.

"She's been questioned," Longshore said. "But I'm not at liberty to say more."

I rolled my eyes. "Of course not. Are you going to look into Linda and Mark Dorsey?"

"It's our duty to follow up on every tip we get," Longshore said.

"But there's really not much there," Randall added.

"Yeah, you've said that," I snapped. "I guess we're done here, then."

"We'll decide when we're done," Longshore said.

I crossed my arms and waited.

He made a show of looking around and then asked Randall, "You satisfied?"

Randall nodded and Longshore said, "We're done here."

"Great," I said with a phony smile. "Have a nice day."

I walked outside behind him, and Hennie tagged along. I stood there with my hands in fists until they drove out of sight. "I can't stand those two!"

Hennie grunted in agreement as Nolan walked in our direction.

"How'd it go?" he asked when he reached us.

"Don't ask."

"That good, huh?" he said.

I gritted my teeth and tried to stop my mind from spinning. "I can't just sit around and wait for them to do nothing. I have to go talk to Linda, no matter how dangerous it might be."

"You're not going alone," Nolan said.

"I'm not being left out of this one," Hennie added.

"Okay," I said. "Then, let's gear up and go."

Chapter 21

The three of us met ten minutes later at my cabin.

"We're all armed?" I asked.

Hennie patted her side holster. Nolan nodded. I had my own handgun tucked into a holster at the center of my lower back.

We got into my truck, and I drove to the address on Mark's business card. He'd mentioned once that his business office was located in his home.

We pulled up to a very white but not overly large house. A sign that said "Dorsey Fireworks" hung over a side door.

A car sat in the driveway, and I thought it looked like Linda's.

"I think she's here." I pointed to the car.

We walked to the front door, and I took my phone from my pocket with shaking hands. I started the audio recorder and slid it back in my pocket. If we managed to get a confession, I wasn't taking any chances that it'd be missed. I knocked and my stomach tumbled as we waited. I steadied myself for what would come. I'd be bold and push hard to get her to confess. There was no other way at this point.

When no one came to the door, I knocked again, louder. We waited and waited.

I walked a few steps into the yard and peeked in the window. No signs of movement except from a cat who walked across the room and stopped to watch me.

"I don't think they're home," I said.

I walked around to the side business entrance. Nolan and Hennie followed, and Nolan knocked on the door loudly. A small sign in the window said "Closed" and the unanswered door backed it up.

I kept walking to the back of the house and looked through the windows again.

Nolan and Hennie trailed along. Hennie peered in through a window beside me. "Nothing," she said.

I knocked on the back door just in case. When no one came, I jiggled the doorknob. It didn't seem especially secure to me, though I didn't have much experience picking locks.

I took my pocket knife out and opened the blade. I worked the tip into the door's jam.

"What do you think you're doing?" Nolan asked.

"I thought if I could get in easily, we could just look around."

"No way. If we break in there, they are within their right to shoot us all."

"But there's no one home, so it's safe." I looked to Hennie for confirmation and she shrugged.

"Anything you find won't be usable in court anyway, so there's no point," he said.

"That's okay. I won't touch anything."

"Then there's no reason to go in."

I jiggled the knife and the door popped open. "It practically opened itself." I shrugged innocently.

Nolan shook his head.

Hennie pulled her sleeves down over her hands. "So we don't leave prints."

I did the same. "See, it's fine."

Nolan crossed his arms. "Aiding and abetting is as far as I go. I'll stand guard out here."

"Even better." I slid behind the door.

"Do not touch anything!" he shouted after Hennie and me.

I paused to look around. It was clear that Linda loved to spend money. Every surface was covered in shiny trinkets and sparkling glass pieces. Somewhere, there was likely a room that no one was allowed in.

I wandered down a short hall to the left, glad that I had on sneakers so that I didn't make noise on the hardwood floors. I found a large powder room and opened the medicine cabinet. Antacid, ibuprofen, anti-itch cream. Nothing of interest jumped out at me.

In the living room, I opened a few drawers in the cabinet under the massive TV. Nothing there, either, that made them look guilty.

"Come up here!" Hennie called to me.

I walked up the stairs, careful not to put my hand on the railing. I found her in the master bedroom with several drawers open in the wooden dresser. The cathedral ceiling and hand-carved woodwork furniture proved further that Linda liked to add expensive touches to everything she could.

Hennie held a box of tampons out to me.

"Uhh, I'm good, thanks."

She sighed. "Don't it seem a little bizarre to you that she keeps her tampons in the bedroom and not the bathroom?"

"Sure. But that doesn't help us prove anything."

"Shows her character."

I shrugged. "I guess. I think we're done here."

Hennie put the tampons back in the dresser before getting to her feet. We crept along the halls and left through the back door.

"Make sure it looks how you found it," Nolan said.

I locked the door and pulled it shut, making sure my sleeve stayed in place over my hand.

We returned to the front of the house and got back in my truck.

"Well, that was a bust," I said. "I really thought we would find something."

"And we didn't get to confront Linda," Nolan said.

"I was looking forward to that," Hennie added.

I turned into the campground entrance and stopped behind a waiting car. "If that turtle is back..."

Nolan jumped out of the truck, craned his neck, and said through the open window, "Turtle is back."

I groaned and turned across the grass into the parking lot. Hennie and I exited the truck and caught up to Nolan in front of the office.

A man stood outside the door with a frustrated look on his face. "Hello? Does anyone work here?"

"I'll see what's going on," I said.

"I'll get the sign," Nolan said.

"And I'll direct traffic until he does," Hennie said.

I walked inside the office and didn't see Sally. I rang up the camper's bread and peanut butter. "Sorry about the wait."

He took his items and left without saying anything.

"Sally?" I walked through the store's aisles. No sign of her.

I opened the door to my office and froze. Linda waited for me, her gun pointed at my face as she perched on the edge of my table desk.

"Shut the door." She slid off the desk.

I kicked the door shut and tried to think of the techniques I knew to disarm someone. I wasn't in a great position for defense.

I held my hands up. "I know you tried to kill me before. You're back to finish things off?"

"Phone." She held her other hand out.

I took my phone from my pocket and placed it in her palm. The instant my hand left hers, I realized I'd missed my chance. I could have grabbed her arm and pulled her toward me, then gotten her into a headlock and forced her to the ground.

My face flushed with the heat of my own stupidity. Why hadn't I thought that through?

"Don't try anything cute," she said. "I sent your registration girl on a goose chase, and that old man is checking on an 'animal attack.'" She curled her lips into a snarl. "We're all alone."

It's okay. It's okay, I told myself. Nolan and Hennie were right outside and knew I was inside. I just had to keep Linda from shooting me until one of them came in.

"What do you want?" I asked.

"You're going to pay for ruining my vacation. Literally." She pointed the gun to the safe and then back to me.

"There's not much in there." I took a step toward the safe.

"I'm sure it's more than what I got from the register last time."

"Are you planning to go on the run?"

She gestured to the safe with the gun. "No questions. Open the safe."

I moved as slowly as I could toward the safe. Behind me, I heard the blessed sound of the door opening and shutting in the store. I let out a sigh of relief as footsteps approached. The door to my office swung open.

When I saw Mark's face instead of Nolan's or Hennie's, I gasped. My body trembled and tears stung my eyes.

"What are you doing?" Mark accused Linda.

I couldn't comprehend his words. What was *she* doing? Wasn't he in on it?

"I'm saving our vacation!" Linda jerked her head toward the door. "Get out of the way, or I'll shoot you!"

"You crazy loon. You'll have to go away and never come back, you do something like this!"

"Fine!" She moved the gun's aim from my face to his. "Then I'll leave your worthless butt and never return. Even better!"

Mark held his hands up. "Put the gun down!"

"Shut up!" she screeched.

I heard the loud pop before I saw Mark's reaction. The bullet hit his arm and knocked him back. He crashed against the wall with a hard thump before stumbling and falling to the floor.

Nolan rushed into the office and threw himself on top of Linda.

"Freeze!" Nolan shouted. Then to me, "Call 9-1-1."

I shot my hand out to grab my phone from where Linda had dropped it on the desk. I could barely dial.

"You're done now!" Mark shouted. "I'm telling them everything!"

"What's your emergency?" the woman on the phone asked me.

"Someone was shot. And we have an armed killer in custody."

The dispatcher was silent for a moment. Then she asked, "What's your location?"

Nolan set Linda's gun on the desk and pinned her arms behind her back.

Hennie appeared in the doorway and jumped into action. She tore the first aid kit from the wall in the main office and pulled out a bandage. I finished giving the dispatcher our address and set my phone down.

Mark howled in pain as Hennie pulled the bandage tight above his wound.

"Gotta stop the bleeding." She pressed another wad of bandages to the gushing hole.

"I should have known," Mark muttered in a half-whine, half-rage. "Linda's been crazy from the start! She made me crazy!"

"She killed Jerry, didn't she?" I asked.

Mark shook his head. "Of course she did! Trying to make you sick." He pointed at me with his other hand.

"Sick? Wasn't she trying to kill me?"

"That's what she claimed. That's why she took my insulin. Eating it makes you sick, so she put it in some muffin you had sitting around."

"But Jerry ate that muffin and died," I said. "Guess she used too much."

"I don't know," he whined and glared at Hennie. "It shouldn't have killed the guy."

"Then why did it?" I asked.

"Why does any of it matter?!" Mark snapped. "If you hadn't cancelled so late, none of this would've happened." He waved his good arm around at the scene, then said to Linda, "You're a goner now. Good riddance!"

Linda's face was pressed against the floor, but she glared at Mark and mumbled, "I'll be back to finish you off!"

"I'd like to see you try!" Mark said.

Sirens blared in the distance. I stepped carefully over Linda and Mark to open the outside office door. Several cops hurried for my office, and I locked the front door behind them so that no campers would come in and witness the scene. I stood there, dumbfounded, as they went to work.

Minutes later, Linda was escorted out of my office in handcuffs. Randall and Longshore held either arm and nearly had to drag her out from behind the front counter.

"I'll see you in hell!" she shouted to Mark.

"Well, it sure wouldn't be heaven if you were there!" he shouted back.

Randall and Longshore took Linda out, and I watched them load her into the back of the cruiser. Once they had her secured, EMTs rushed in and tended to Mark. He was taken out handcuffed to a stretcher a short time later, with two cops following closely behind.

The ambulance and the cruiser Linda was in drove off, and Detective Hooley approached me. "I know you usually talk to Officers Longshore and Randall," he said. "But since they're busy, I thought I'd talk to you myself."

"Happily."

I gave Hooley the details of everything that happened, starting with the moment I entered my office and saw Linda.

"Maybe it wasn't premeditated if she only tried to make me sick and not kill me," I admitted. "But she must've used too much insulin in the muffin and it killed Jerry."

Hooley narrowed his eyes. "I don't think that's possible. Stomach acid would neutralize the insulin. I only have paramedic training, so I can't say for sure, but I'm fairly certain."

"Then why...?" I dug back in my mind to my first conversation with Barbara. What had she told me? "Jerry did have a stomach condition. Hypochlora-something? It made him have low stomach acid."

Hooley nodded. "That might have contributed to his death. The autopsy should tell us more when the final results come back."

"Even if she wasn't planning to kill me, everyone heard Mark say she killed Jerry, and the whole thing is on video. That should be enough to get a conviction."

"I should hope so." He flipped his notebook closed and tucked it in his pocket. "That's all I need for now." He walked off to find Hennie.

I took my phone out and tapped the screen quickly as Nolan came over to me.

"How you holding up?" he asked.

I sucked in a breath and pushed it out. "Tired. Glad it's over."

He pointed to my phone. "Too bad you didn't get the whole thing on that audio recording."

"Uhh... Yeah..." I slid the phone back into my pocket. "Did you?"

"Maybe? It doesn't matter because the police have the video footage from the office. That's much more valuable in court than an audio-only recording. And I just deleted it, so it's gone forever now anyhow."

Realization washed over his face and he smirked. "And also because the audio recording has evidence of your little felony."

"Shh!" I looked around, but no one stood near us. "I have no idea what you're talking about." I pushed my nose into the air and put a hand on my hip.

"You know I don't like it when you get sloppy."

"I cleaned everything up, so no worries."

"We've had too many close calls lately." Nolan wrapped his arms around me and held me tight. His warmth and closeness soaked into me, comforting me. We stood there for several long minutes.

"I want to go to bed and wake up tomorrow like none of this ever happened," I said.

"Then I'll walk you home."

"There's one thing we have to do first." I looked behind me to the gathering of women standing by the goat pen, watching me intently. They'd been waiting a long time for an update.

We walked over to them, and I said, "I'm happy to tell you all that Jerry's killer is in police custody."

The women cheered and hugged each other. One of them said, "Thank you for all your hard work. Sally told us how much you've done to bring him justice. I hope that witch goes away for a long time for what she did."

"I think she will."

Nolan and I turned and walked away as they continued celebrating. He weaved his fingers between mine and led the way to my cabin. On my doorstep, he held me for a long while before kissing me.

"You want me to stay?" he asked.

"I think I'm okay. Especially now that Linda is out of the picture. I'm so tired, hopefully I'll just crash."

"Big day tomorrow," he said.

I nodded. "We've been working on this event for weeks now."

"That, and you're meeting my family."

"Right." My throat tightened. Were we ready for that?

He pulled his mouth into a crooked smile. "They'll love you."

He kissed me once more before walking off toward his camper. I went inside, wondering if I would sleep at all that night.

Chapter 22

I kneeled on my front porch to tie a red, white, and blue bandana around Gar's neck. I stood to inspect him. "Perfect. You look very festive."

He barked his approval, and we walked down to Nolan's camper. We passed the new pond, and I squinted at the object near it. I felt a surge of joy when I realized it was the turtle. She was close to the pond, apparently having come from the nest. The plan had worked.

We continued on and I smelled the food before we reached Nolan's site. My stomach growled in response. Gar ran ahead of me and dashed around to the back of the camper.

When I rounded the corner, I saw Nolan at the grill and Andre and Jake playing with Gar.

"Just in time," Nolan said when he saw me.

He scraped eggs from a griddle onto four paper plates, then used tongs to set a plump sausage on each.

"Now that's breakfast," Andre said.

No one spoke as we devoured the food. When we'd finished, I collected the plates and took them inside to toss them in the trash. Nolan stepped inside behind me.

"I just wanted to say this before the day gets crazy." He took my hand, and the look in his eyes made my heart skip.

I squeezed his hand back and waited. His expression was so stern and serious that I felt a jolt of fear, though I couldn't imagine what he was about to say.

"I know what I said last night about meeting my family and everything," he said. "I don't want to rush things. You don't have to meet them if you don't want to. And if you do, it doesn't mean anything. What we have is casual, and that's the way it'll stay."

"Oh, okay." I squeezed his hand but struggled to swallow through the disappointment. I didn't have much reason to feel let down when he was giving me exactly what I'd said I wanted. He didn't know I'd been slowly changing my mind. The problem was, I didn't know if this meant *he* wanted things to stay casual or if he was just doing it for my sake. "I've been looking forward to meeting your family. I hope you get to meet mine soon, too."

"Great." He looked relieved as he smiled. "Point me in the direction you want me, and I'll get to work."

I took a deep breath and tried to push aside the new weight in my chest. We had too much going on for me to be distracted by trying to figure out our relationship.

"We have the decorations to put up first and the tables to get into place," I said. "The food will go on later, but the video screen should be set up early so we can test it. I think it takes time to blow the screen up."

He nodded, and we walked back out onto the deck.

"If there's anything we can do to help," Jake said, "I'd be glad."

Andre nodded. "I'm grateful to have a place like this to go. You don't find too many quiet Fourth of July events."

I smiled. "I'm glad we could do it. And we can always use extra eyes and muscle for security. The police may have the killer in custody, but Linda isn't the only source of danger out there. We also need to make sure no one sneaks fireworks in."

"Absolutely," Jake said.

Andre added, "We're on it."

Nolan and I said goodbye to them and walked to the rec hall with Gar leading the way.

We spent the morning getting things moved and setup. Before I knew it, noon had arrived, more people were out and about, and it was time to get the food ready for the event to start.

I carried a box of hotdog buns over to where Nolan had fired up the grill. As I neared him, I froze. Four adults and two children stood around Nolan, talking and laughing. I could tell instantly who they were. Nolan and his brother both looked a lot like their dad.

Nolan saw me and waved me over. "Thea, meet my parents, brother, sister-in-law, niece, and nephew."

I smiled, shook their hands, and tried to remember all six names.

Nolan's mother took my hand in both of hers. "We know you're busy, so we'll talk another time, but it's so good to meet you."

"You too." I returned her warm smile.

Nolan beamed at me. I wanted to feel more excited for the moment, or to say something meaningful, or to not feel like I wanted to run, but his words kept cycling through my mind. *What we have is still casual, and that's the way it'll stay.* If it was so casual, I didn't want to get attached to his family.

I smiled again and thanked them all for coming as I excused myself. I turned and caught Hennie watching. I bolted through the thickening crowd to avoid her.

In the office, I opened the box of turtle-name entries and went through them. There was everything from Pokey, Sparkle, and Flash to Bob, Jerry, and Sally. Well, I certainly wasn't going to name the turtle after my employee. I narrowed it down to my top three, then chose at random. I tucked the winning slip in my pocket and walked back outside to make sure the cupcake table was ready.

As I stepped onto the main road, Kimberly pulled into the parking lot in her pink and white van. I waited, then led her and her helper to the rec hall.

"So, I heard they got the killer," Kimberly whispered.

"Yup, last night."

"I can't believe it wasn't Barbara."

"Me either. But I don't think she's innocent. Detective Hooley said they were getting a warrant for her arrest."

Kimberly shivered and continued setting cupcakes on the display tower. Hennie walked in and I waved her over.

"Want to help me judge the decoration contest?" I asked her.

"If we can take my four-wheeler."

I nodded. "That would make it go much faster. Curtis is out on the golf cart."

Hennie and I climbed onto her four-wheeler, and she drove us slowly through the looping campground roads. Many sites had been decked out with patriotic decorations.

"Wait a second," I said.

We stopped in front of one site that was over the top. Strings of red, white, and blue rope lights ran around the top of the camper and the food canopy. Several large tissue-paper balls hung from the lights. Spinning foil decorations filled the ground in front of the camper, beside the large wooden cutout of Uncle Sam. To top it all off, a large USA flag covered the front of the camper.

I snapped a photo of site 45. A woman came out of the camper and hurried over to us.

"Just a minute! We're not quite done."

I looked at the older woman in her blue shorts with white stars and red-and-white-striped top. She wore a red-rimmed hat with more stars, this time in silver glitter. As we waited, sound erupted from the camper. "God Bless the USA" played from inside. The woman's husband, dressed in a similar fashion, came out to join her.

"It's not complete without the music," he explained.

The couple held hands and gazed at their work with satisfaction.

"I'd say this site has a pretty good chance of winning," I told them. "No one else did half as much."

"We're a little worried about site 104," the woman said.

The husband whistled and nodded. "They have a blowup Sam."

I raised my eyebrows at Hennie and took a photo of the couple in front of their camper before we headed off. We drove through the rest of the campground, and when we reached the back of the main loop, I saw what site 45 had been worried about.

Site 104 was a tent site, but they hadn't let that fact keep them from filling every inch of the space with something Americana. They also had lights, which bordered the tent and picnic table. There was the inflatable Uncle Sam, as mentioned, and there were many little flags lining a path to the tent.

I looked at Hennie and scratched my head. "These are definitely the top two."

I snapped some photos and we drove off.

"I'm thinking the music set 45 over the top," Hennie said.

I nodded. "I want to get a few more votes so we're not biased."

By the time we got back to the front of the campground, it was late afternoon. People were scattered everywhere, and I saw that someone had moved the turtle sign near where she was at the moment—a few feet from the new pond. The agent from the MDC had set up a table with flyers near the nest and was standing by, answering questions and sharing turtle facts. The local band I'd hired was setting up to play for the next few hours.

Hennie had gone off to work on the video screen for later, and I was making rounds from the rec hall to the office to the pavilion, checking on everyone, when Enid waved to me.

"Yoo hoo!"

She must've saved her most festive cardigan for today. This one was knitted like a giant flag stretched from the top of her shoulders to her knees.

"Happy Fourth of July," I said and gave her a quick hug.

"This event is looking fabulous, but there's someone you need to see in the office."

"Oh. Thanks." I wasn't sure who she could mean, but I headed that way.

When I walked in, I saw two familiar but unexpected faces. I gasped in surprise.

"Mom? Dad?"

They turned from their conversation with Curtis and Rose, and my mom let out a squeal when she saw me.

"Oh Thea, you've done a wonderful job here," she said, hugging me hard.

"It's good to see the place so packed," my dad added after giving me his own hug.

"Thanks. It's been a lot of work. I'm glad you could come and see it." My heart swelled with pride and excitement. I'd been disappointed when it seemed none of my family would come. And though I wanted him to meet my parents, I felt vividly aware of the fact that Nolan was just outside, and his family was wandering around somewhere out there, too. My mom and dad had no idea I was seeing someone—no matter how casual it might or might not be.

"I see Enid is still going strong," my mom said. "And Curtis was just telling us about the last season your grandparents had here together. I do miss them." She smiled sadly.

"It's still weird sometimes being here without them," I said. "But in some ways, it's like they never left."

She gave me another hug. "So good to see you."

There was no point in putting the meeting off. How could I tell her about Nolan, though, without having her make a big deal of it? "There's someone I want you to meet."

They didn't seem to suspect anything as I led them outside to the pavilion where Nolan was manning the grill. His father and brother stood with him, talking.

This was a mistake. They couldn't all meet each other, could they? I considered turning back, but it was too late. Nolan saw us.

My heart thumped louder with each step. I smiled at Nolan and gestured toward my parents. "My mom and dad decided to surprise me."

Nolan raised his eyebrows and set down his flipper. I caught a fleeting look of panic in his eyes, but he covered it with a polite smile as he shook their hands. "So nice to meet you both."

Once everyone had been introduced, I stood there, awkwardly, not knowing what else to say.

My mother whispered to me, "I didn't know we were meeting a *man*! He's cute!" She beamed and patted my arm.

I needed an excuse to get out, fast. "I hate to leave you all, but I have a bunch of things to take care of." I felt a little bad about leaving Nolan alone with them, but I wasn't exaggerating.

"Need any help?" my dad asked.

"I got it. Thanks. You just hang out and enjoy the event."

"Then don't let us get in your way," my mom added.

I walked away, grateful to be leaving the uncomfortable situation. When I glanced over my shoulder, I caught them all laughing at something. My family and Nolan's family, together and getting to know each other. This should be a good thing, I reminded myself. But Nolan's insistence that this "doesn't mean anything" felt like a heavy rain cloud over the significant moment.

When the day turned to evening and the light faded, I addressed the crowd. I turned the music down low and stood on a chair at the edge of the large pavilion.

"Welcome everyone and happy Fourth of July! I have a few announcements to make." I took out the piece of paper I'd stuck in my pocket earlier. "We had two contests going on. First, the decorating contest." I saw the couple from site 45 clutching hands and looking hopeful. I smiled at them. "The winner is site number 45, with site 104 in second place." The couple jumped and clapped in delight as the crowd applauded.

A few feet from the happy couple of site 45, a man threw his blue cap to the ground and stomped. "I thought for sure the Sam would do it," he complained to his wife.

"Second place isn't bad." She patted his shoulder, and he glowered at the ground.

I moved on before a fight could break out over who had more mini flags. "We also had a contest to name our special visitor, the female alligator snapping turtle who laid eggs in our horseshoe pit." I opened the scrap of paper. "The winning name is Holly, suggested by camper Julie Schwimmer." I looked out over the cheering crowd.

I saw a young girl, maybe eight or nine, bouncing in excitement and giving high fives to her family. Sally stood nearby, shooting an unhappy look Julie's way. I felt bad I hadn't picked Sally's name, but I couldn't bring myself to have a turtle named Princess creeping around the place.

"The new pond will be named Holly Pond, since it was built for her. Thank you to everyone who entered the contests. The fireworks display will take place on that large screen in just a little while. Thank you all for coming, and I hope you have a safe and quiet Fourth."

I stepped down from the chair, intending to go check on things in the office. Instead, I was stopped by several people who came to thank me.

One man shook my hand hard. "I appreciate you doing this quiet thing. I'm never able to celebrate the Fourth with my family, but this year, we'll all be together." A woman stood proudly at his side, and three small children played with a ball nearby.

"I'm so glad," I said and turned to the next family.

"This is a great idea," the woman said. "We need more safe places like this." She leaned in closer to me so her preteen kids wouldn't hear. "I usually have to self medicate so heavily that I miss the holiday completely."

I put my hand on her shoulder. "I'm glad you could be here."

Inside the office, Sally stood slumped over, elbows on the counter, with a sour look on her face. A few campers roamed around the store.

"Has it been busy?" I asked.

She pushed her hair back and nodded. "It's been almost non-stop. I just stepped outside to hear the winners since it finally died down."

"I'm sorry I didn't pick your name. I liked it, I just thought Holly fit better."

Sally stood up. "It's okay. That's not what I'm upset about."

"Oh. What's wrong?"

She reached under the counter and pulled out her Bishop purse. The yellow leather of the pointed end was torn into shreds.

I gasped. "What happened to it?"

Sally wiped her eyes and put the purse back under the counter. "Those boys." She forced a laugh, but it didn't come close to sounding genuine.

"Oh, no. What'd they do?"

"They were playing pretend and thought it looked like a piece of pizza."

I gulped and felt my eyes widen. She didn't know I'd thought the same thing when I saw it.

"They fed it to the neighbor's dog." She burst into sobs and covered her face with her hands.

I rubbed her back and smiled awkwardly at the nearby camper watching us.

"I know how much that purse meant to you," I said.

"I worked so hard to save up enough!" she whined. "And now that Jerry is gone forever and Barbara is going to jail, no one knows what will happen to the purses!"

Sally's shoulders shook as she cried into my arm. Several minutes passed before she straightened up and wiped her eyes.

"Do you want to take a minute?" I asked.

She shook her head resolutely. "No, I'm not going to let them get to me this time."

"Are the twins here? I haven't seen them."

"They're on punishment," she bragged.

I knew Sally couldn't often bring herself to discipline her boys. Likely the reason they were so crazy to begin with. If she'd made them stay home and miss the event, she must really be angry.

"I'm sorry for your loss." I patted her arm. "Let me know if I can do anything."

She smiled sadly. "Just let me know if you hear of any Bishops for sale. I've decided to take the money for a new one from the boys' college fund."

I almost choked holding back my laughter. Good for her to take a stand for once. "I sure will."

I left the office and went to check on the video screen. Hennie and Nolan had blown it up and staked it down. We rented a projector for my laptop, which Nolan set up and tested out earlier.

"Everything going okay?" I asked.

Nolan nodded. "Ready to start."

When full night hit, Nolan started the video, and Hennie hit play on the sound system. The fireworks exploded silently in sync with "The Star-Spangled Banner." The crowd oo'ed and ah'ed with the blasts, and some folks sang along to the music.

I stood to watch a little while, feeling relief for the first time that the event had gone well and was now nearing its end. I regretted that I hadn't spent much time with my parents, but I knew they were enjoying themselves around the campground. We'd had the best times together here over the years, and I'd see them more tomorrow.

Nolan walked over and took my hand. "Hennie can finish this up. Take a walk with me?"

The mischievous glint in his eyes made my stomach flutter. What was he up to? I glanced behind me at the people spread over the grass in chairs or on blankets, watching the display. "I'd love to."

We walked away from the crowd, and the night grew darker as we entered a wooded section. Nolan led me through the trees until we reached a small clearing that was made private by the trees and brush. In the center of the clearing was the picnic he'd set up for us.

"What's all this?" I asked.

He sat on the blanket and patted the spot beside him. "I'm starving and I'll guess you didn't eat, either."

"I've picked at some things here and there." I gave him a fake glare. "You're telling me you didn't eat while you were grilling?"

"I only had a few burgers and some cupcakes, and that was hours ago." He unzipped a small fabric cooler and took out several cold burgers. "I also snuck this." He showed me a bottle of red wine. "To celebrate."

I sat beside him, eating my cold burger and sipping wine from the bottle.

"This has been the best Fourth of July I can remember in a long time," he said. "After the force and then a few years in the war..." He stared off at the stars for a moment.

"It must've been difficult for you," I said.

"It was."

"You don't talk about it much."

He took my hand and held my gaze for a long while. "I know I haven't been as open with you as you've been with me. I guess I couldn't see getting into all that if this wasn't going anywhere."

"You don't think it is?" My stomach skipped as I waited for his answer.

"Well, I don't know. I'm hopeful, but I know you need to take things slow and keep it casual. It's hard to balance the two."

"Is that what you want? To keep things casual?" I looked down at our twined fingers.

"I just want a peaceful life with whatever happiness I can find. If that means we have to take things real slow, then I can do that."

"But what if it's not what I want anymore?"

He raised his eyebrows. "What are you saying? You don't want to be in a relationship at all?"

"No. I mean, what if I want us to make our relationship... less casual?"

"Oh." He nodded, then grinned. "That works for me."

I felt immense relief and a flash of excitement. But one thing still needed to be resolved. "There's something I have to ask you. It's been bugging me for a while."

"Okay."

I bit my lip, afraid to hear his response. "I need to know why you were fired from the police force."

He sat back and looked surprised. "That's what you need to know? Not why I was discharged from the Marines?"

"I didn't know you were discharged from the Marines." The rock in my stomach grew.

"I was only active for two years. It's usually a four-year commitment."

My chest tightened. Being fired from being a cop was bad enough, but being discharged from the military could carry significant consequences. They didn't kick people out for nothing.

"Then I guess there are two things I need to know," I said.

"The police force..." He blew out a long breath. "What finally did it wasn't anything I saw coming." He squeezed my hand. "A lot of city cops are crooked, you know. But even the straight ones take handouts from time to time. I was tempted on a few occasions. Easy money, no one would know, and all I had to do was turn my back on a little crime and pretend like I didn't see anything."

I swallowed hard. I wanted him to talk faster, to tell me the worst part so I would know if I could live with it or not.

"I couldn't bring myself to do it, though," he continued, "and eventually, that caused me some problems. Other cops don't like it when you don't go along with what they want. I uncovered a huge bribery scheme with one of the gangs in the city. This wasn't a little gang doing misdemeanors, either. Murders were being covered up, along with lesser crimes like vandalism, physical assault, burglary. I didn't want to let it go on. I wanted to stop that gang and clean up the streets. It wasn't long before that—"

He sucked in a shaky breath, and I could see the pain in his eyes as he continued.

"Before that, I had messed up an arrest. One little step out of order and the defense attorney got him off on a technicality. A murderer walked and then he killed again—a little girl—and it always felt like my fault that she died. It was a stupid mistake."

He chewed his lip for a moment, and I put my other hand on his back.

He finally went on. "After that, I wasn't going to let anyone get away. But when I started making arrests within the gang, two officers came to me and tried to get me to buy in. If I took the money and did nothing, everything would be fine. I just had to be okay with the guilt. Well, I wasn't. I planned to come forward and not only stop the bribery, but also these cops who went too far. I guess I'm lucky to be alive."

He shook his head and took a long sip of the wine.

"I'm grateful I was fired," he finally said. "It got me out of that situation with a nice little severance, and the cops I was trying to expose no longer had a reason to want me dead. I walked away quietly and tried to pretend that I didn't know about the reality of what was going on. But that became too much, so I joined the

Marines to have a way to make a difference. To save lives."

He stopped and looked up at the stars again. "But that was a bad idea."

I waited patiently, not sure what to feel. So far, it sounded better than I hoped, but we weren't at the end yet.

"What happened when you joined the military?" I asked when it seemed like he wouldn't say more.

"It became too much. The stress and the trauma from 12 years of police work, then going off and seeing that war." He closed his eyes and rubbed his forehead. "They sent me home after two years because they were afraid I was going to flip out and kill someone."

"So, it was a medical discharge?"

He nodded. "For PTSD, officially. But really, it was that I couldn't control my anger."

I blinked at him in shock. "You couldn't control it? You don't seem like an angry person to me." The few times I'd seen him mad were exceptional circumstances where we'd been fighting a killer.

"That's why I'm here. Not much to make me mad when I'm surrounded by nature." He gestured to the trees. "Hunting and fishing is good for my soul."

"Grandad used to always say, 'It's hard to worry—and fish.'"

He chuckled. "True. I'm also on a medication that helps me sleep. I'm better when I sleep well and exercise a lot. It's great having a physical job."

"I have medication, too," I admitted. "I take it as needed when something comes up. Though, the pills make me sleepy, so I don't take them often. And I was in therapy before I moved."

"I've done that, too. It's hard to find a therapist who gets what I've been through."

"I bet." I let a few moments of silence pass before I asked the question burning in my mind. "When you said you got fired, you didn't really say what for exactly."

He clenched his jaw, and his eyes tightened as he took a moment to answer. "They set me up. The cops I wanted to expose. They made me look like the crooked one. Said I took bribes. I didn't fight it because I wanted out. My chief was good enough to me that he dropped the charges later. He knew what was really going on. But anyone who looks into it will see that Nolan Cade was fired for accepting bribes. Not exactly something I want people to believe about me."

"There's nothing you can do to clear your name?"

"It's not worth it. Some things are better left alone."

"I get that. I have the same attitude about things with Russell. I could've sued him and got back some of my money, but the stress of going through that…"

"Sanity is more important than money."

"I guess that's why I'm here."

"It's the perfect escape for both of us." He kissed my hand. "That's why I didn't want to tell you any of that and take the chance that you might see me differently."

"I do. But not in a bad way. We've both been through a lot."

He nodded slowly. "I'm grateful for what I have now. For what we have. I want my life to be simple. Fulfilling, but without the trauma. Being here and having this... whatever we have—is exactly what I want out of life."

"Me too." My heart raced with the words I wanted to say next. "And if we can keep it simple, I want to make this more serious."

"I don't know how good I am at either of those things, but I'd like to try."

"I'm not even sure what 'more serious' looks like," I admitted, "but we've met each other's family now and that feels more serious."

"My parents are already asking when we can come for a visit."

"Oh, boy." I laughed. "I haven't talked to mine since they met you. They didn't know I was seeing someone. I'll never hear the end of it."

"Thea, whatever you want this to be, I'm on board. I don't want to complicate things, but I really like being with you. It feels right."

"I agree. And I think..." I swallowed hard and wished I could stop my palms from sweating. "I think I'm ready to try..."

He raised an eyebrow and waited.

I squeezed my eyes shut and blurted, "I want to make things physical, but I'm terrified."

He put a hand to my cheek, and I opened my eyes to meet his sympathetic gaze.

"I know," he said. "Don't feel like you have to. It's fine. Really."

"It's not. I've been going crazy for weeks. I can't look at you in your running gear, I can't watch you fix things, I can't even watch you walk away from me without wanting to rip your clothes off."

He laughed. "I had no idea I was torturing you so much."

"Well, stop being so sexy then." I stuck my tongue out at him.

"If that would make things easier for you, I'd try, but..." He flexed his large bicep. "I just don't see how it would be possible to turn this off."

I rolled my eyes. "I've created a monster."

He gave me a silly grin and leaned in close. He whispered, "If you feel the need to rip my clothes off, I won't object."

I breathed out nervously. "Maybe not quite that physical."

He leaned in and kissed me hard. "Tell me what you need."

I let my fingers trace the contours of his chest and felt my blood racing. "I need you."

A soft explosion in the sky made us look up. In the distance, a fireworks display had started. The sound was far enough away to not disturb our night or the event. We watched for a moment, the warmth of his arms around me, giving me the comfort and confidence I needed.

I turned and wrapped my arms around his neck to kiss him. This time, I didn't pull away when things started heating up. With the flash of the fireworks lighting our way, we melted into each other and left the pains of our pasts behind us so we could move into the future, together.

Note from the Author

Thank you so much for reading ONE BODY SHORT OF A PICNIC. I hope you enjoyed your time with Thea and her crew. I had a blast writing it, and I can't wait to get back there!

Would you consider leaving a review?

Reviews are a huge help to indie authors like me. I'd be grateful if you would give just a few minutes of your time to let others know what you thought of the book. Reviews not only help other readers find the books they're looking for, they help indie authors get seen.

Leave a review:
ZoeyChase.com/OneBodyShortOfAPicnic

Thank you!
Zoey Chase

Find out more about how Gar came to Cedar Fish Campground in the short story "Fishy Beginnings."

When Gar's secret past is discovered, Thea must fight to keep her beloved pet.

Gar, a black Newfoundland puppy, mysteriously showed up at Cedar Fish Campground and became the perfect companion to heal Thea's grief-stricken, dog-loving heart. With such a serendipitous beginning, Thea never questioned the life Gar had before he found her. But one newspaper article could change everything.

Thea discovers a secret about Gar that could mean she loses him forever. With help from her ex-cop security guard, Nolan, and her quirky sidekick, Hennie, Thea must draw on her past to win the right to keep Gar before she loses another treasured pet.

FISHY BEGINNINGS is a short story that takes place after the events of *Between a Rock and a Deadly Place*, book one in the Cedar Fish Campground Series. If you love dogs or have ever lost a pet, you'll love this tale of hilarious animal antics and moments that will both break and warm your pet-loving heart.

**Get the story FREE
when you join my mailing list!**

ZoeyChase.com/FishyBeginnings

About the Author

Zoey Chase received her MFA in creative writing from Carlow University. She lives in the Pittsburgh area with her husband, three daughters, three cats, and vast book collection. Can usually be found doing something bookish.

www.ZoeyChase.com
Facebook: /AuthorZoeyChase
Instagram: @AuthorZoeyChase